iPhone 13 User Guide

The Most Complete and Intuitive Step-by-Step Manual to Master your New iPhone 13, with Tips and Tricks for Senior Beginner Users

Adam Norton

Copyright 2022 © Adam Norton

All rights reserved. No part of this publication may be reproduced or distributed in any form or by any means, electronic or mechanical, including photocopying, recording, or by any information storage or retrieval system, without the prior written consent of the author.

ISBN:

Table of Contents

Introduction 1

Chapter 1. Introduction and Terminology 4

    The iPhone 13 Features 4

        Sizes 5

        Design 6

        Display 7

        Storage Space 7

        Water Resistance 8

        RAM 8

        Color Range 8

Chapter 2. The Most Important Things to Know 9

    The iOS 11

    Display 11

    Camera 11

    A15 Bionic Processor 12

    Battery 12

    Final Verdict on the New Features 12

Chapter 3. Let's Start With Your iPhone 13

    Set Up and Get Started 13

        Step 1: Connect Your iPhone 13

        Step 2: Set Up iCloud Backup 13

        Step 3: Set Up iCloud Backup on Your iPhone 14

        Step 4: Set Up Passbook 14

        Step 5: Manage Your Apple ID 14

        Step 6: Manage Photos 14

        Step 7: Manage iWork 15

Step 8: Manage App Store Purchases 15
Step 9: Manage iCloud 15
Step 10: Manage iCloud Backup 15
Step 11: Manage Documents and Data 16
How to Set Up Cellular Service 16
How to Connect Your Phone to a Wi-Fi Network on iPhone 13 17
How to Set Up Cellular Service 17
How to Check Data Usage and Battery Levels 18
How to Enable/Disable Your Device 18
How to Turn on the Location Services 18
How to Enable/Disable the Mobile Data/Wi-Fi Hotspot 19
How to Activate or Deactivate iCloud Data 19

Chapter 4. Let's Start With the Basics Together 20

Wake iPhone 20
Open Your Device Using Face ID 21
Open Your iPhone With the Login Code 22
Unlock Your iPhone With Your Apple Watch 22
Insert a Nano SiM 22
Basic Gestures 24
Put Your Device In Silent Mode 28
Launch Applications on Your Device 28
Remove Applications From Your Device 30
Find Settings on Your Device 31
Use and Personalize the Control Centre 32
To Access More Controls in the Control Center 33
To Add and Arrange Controls 34
Disable Access to the Controls Center in Applications 34
Connect to and Disconnect From a WiFi Network 34
Set the Date and Time 34
Change the Sounds and Vibration 34
Activate or Deactivate Haptic Feedback 35

Set Your Language & Region on Your Device 35
Rename Your iPhone 36
Change Your Wallpaper 36
Use a Live Picture as Your Wallpaper 37
Use the Display Zoom to Magnify the iPhone Display 38
Activate or Deactivate Dark Mode 38
    Schedule Dark Mode to Activate & Deactivate Automatically 38
Adjust the Screen Brightness Manually 39
Automatically Adjust the Brightness of the Screen 39
Enable or Disable True Tone 39
Activate or Deactivate Night Shift 39
Access Features From Your Device Lock Screen 40
Take a Screenshot 40
Capture a Full-Page Screenshot 41
Record Your iPhone Screen 41
Change or Lock the Screen Orientation 42
Arrange Applications in Folders 42
    To Create a Folder 43
Transfer Applications on Your Home Screen 43
Hide and Display the Home Screen Page 44
Multitask Using Picture in Picture 45
Dictate Text on Your Device 46
    To Dictate 47
    Select & Edit the Text 47
Store Keystrokes Using Text Replacements 49
Add or Change Keyboards on Your iPhone 49
Switch to Another Keyboard 50
Use Another Keyboard Layout 50
AirDrop 50
    To Send Things Via Airdrop 51
    Allowing Others to Send Stuff to Your Device Via Airdrop 51

Draw in Applications Using Markup 51
    Draw Using Markup 52
    To Erase an Error 53
Perform Quick Actions From the Home Screen & the Application Library 53
Live Text 55
Visual Look Up 56
Set an Alarm 57
Use the Compass on Your Device 58
Automatically Update iPhone 58
Upgrade Your iPhone Manually 59
Measure Someone's Height 59
Use Your Device Like a Scale 60

Chapter 5. Apps and App Store 62

Explore the App Store 62
    Download and Purchase Apps 62
    Hide a Purchased App 63
    Update Installed Apps 63
    Re-Download an Uninstalled App 63
    Uninstall an App 64
    Lots of Games to Play With Your Friends on the iPhone 64
iTunes App 64
    Listen to Songs 65
    Share Music Library With Others 65
    Search for Content 65
Find My App 65
    Add Your iPhone 66
    Add a Device Belonging to a Family Member 67
Music App 67
    How to Purchase Apple Music 68
    How to Download Songs From Apple Music 69

Chapter 6. Camera 70

Camera Interface 70

Camera Settings 71

    ISO 71

    Shutter Speed 72

    Focus 72

    Autofocus 72

How to Use the Camera to Take Still Photos 73

    How to Use Live Focus 73

    How to Use Portrait Mode 74

    How to Take Pano Pictures 74

How to Take a Screenshot 74

    Take a Screenshot With Gestures 75

    Using Screen Recorder 75

    How to Record Screen on iPhone 13 Series 75

How to Take Videos 76

How to Scan QR Code With Your Camera 76

How to Use Picture-in-Picture 77

    How to Control Volume 79

Chapter 7. Music, Video, and the Latest News 80

News 80

Apple, iPhone, and Entertainment 81

Some Applications Within the Apple Ecosystem for Video, Music, and News 82

App Music 83

Splice 84

iMovie 84

Chapter 8. Web and Communication 86

Safari 86

    Weather 87

    How to Disable Safari's Website Tinting 87

Quickly Refresh Safari Web Page 88
How to Customize the Start Page and Background of Safari 89
Delete Tabs Group 90
How to Make Your IP Address Untraceable 90
FaceTime 90
Set Up iPhone FaceTime 90
Receive a FaceTime Call 91
Start a Facetime Conversation Call From Messages 92
Submit a Message 92
Call Again 92
FaceTime Sound Settings 92
View FaceTime Participants in a Grid Structure 93
Create a Link to a FaceTime Call 94

Chapter 9. Utilities and Maps App 95

Using Maps 95
What Is Apple Maps App? 96
Google Maps 97
Downloading the Google Maps for iPhone App 97
How to Share Your Location 98
Calculating the Location of an Address 99
How to Set up Voice Mail 99

Chapter 10. Health and Fitness 101

Health 101
Add Health Data to iPhone Manually 102
Monitor Walking Steadiness 103
Get Notifications for Low or Very Poor Steadiness 103
See Your Data for Walking Steadiness 104
See Health Trends 104
View Highlights 105
Create Memoji 106
Send Memoji Stickers 106
Memoji Recordings and Animated Memoji 107

Configure iPhone Focus 107
    Set Focus 107
Check Weather Conditions 109
    How to Read Full-Screen Air Quality, Precipitation, and Temperature Maps
    110
Organize Reminder Lists 111
    Creating, Editing, or Deleting Lists and Groups 111
    Use Tags 111

Chapter 11. Siri 113

How to Instruct Siri to Control Your HomeKit Devices at a
Predetermined Time 114
How to Use Siri While Not Connected 115
How to Make Siri Read Your Notifications 115

Chapter 12. Setting Troubleshooting 117

Using a Computer Backup, Restore Your iPhone 117
How to Update iOS 117
How to Restart Your Device 118
How to Force Restart 119

Chapter 13. Tips and Tricks 120

A Revamped Design 120
Prioritize Your Downloads 120
Rearrange How You Share Your Write-Ups 120
Drag Sketches Within Your Message 121
Change the Capturing Path in Panoramas 121
Pressure Delicate Display 121
Look for Words While Browsing 122
Bring Shortcuts for Emojis 122
Require Arbitrary Passwords From Siri 122
Adjust the Flashlight 122
Cellular and Photovoltaic Charger 123

Correct Siri's Pronunciation 123
Make Use of the Camera's Depth of Field 123
Established Music on the Timer 123
Make Quick Videos 124
Photo in Apple ProRAW 124
Get the MagSafe Portfolio Case With Find My Support 124
Voice Web Search 125
Identify Animals, Articles, and Plants in the Photos 125
Use New Clothing Options for Memoji 125
Tip on How to Make Use of Your Camera to Scan Texts 125
Watch Videos in Picture-in-Picture Mode 126
Change the Default Browser 126

Conclusion 127

Introduction

The iPhone 13 is a smartphone released by Apple on June 19, 2018. This guide is meant to help you if you need tips for new features in the iPhone 13 and to provide answers to any questions that you may have about the phone.

The smartphone has a 6.1-inch display with a resolution of 1792x828p and an A13 Bionic chip inside it—meaning it has very high processing power and is much faster than older models of iPhones. The iPhone also has improved cameras, including dual 12MP wide-angle and telephoto cameras on the backside, as well as a 7MP front-facing camera on the front side for selfies.

The iPhone 13 comes in gold, silver, and grey colors to match your style and preference. Even though the phone was just released, it already has some technology that is advanced for its time. The phone allows you to face unlock and use the TrueDepth camera system to secure the phone without needing an Apple Watch or a passcode. With depth-sensing technology, you can have Face ID on the iPhone 13 wherever you are using your iPhone with an active TrueDepth camera system. The TrueDepth camera system also allows users to send better messages by animating handwritten notes using augmented reality with augmented reality features such as AR Emoji.

The iPhone 13 has both a home button and fingerprint sensor on the back of the phone to allow easy interaction with iPhone features such as touch ID, voice control, and messaging features. The backside of the iPhone also has a beautiful design with glass covering full-view camera lenses for clear images and you can choose screen protectors specially designed for your iPhone from AppleCare or buy one from third-party companies that are made just for your smartphone.

This guide is meant to provide tips on how to use your new smartphone so please read it carefully to prevent any problems.

How Do I Use the iPhone 13?

The iPhone 13 is a great smartphone that comes with lots of helpful features. You can find out how to use the new features on your phone through the available tutorial, in-depth guides, and release notes. You can also visit apple's official website for more information, or you can ask your friends and family who have experience using iPhones or search online for video tutorials from third-party companies that provide iOS tips.

How Do I Unlock My iPhone 13?

The new iPhones allow users to unlock their phones using a facial recognition system called Face ID instead of using fingerprints or passcodes to unlock their phones. Face ID allows users to unlock the phone with a single touch on the face by using facial features and motion detectors inside the phone so that it knows who is holding the phone.

Face ID can be used in different environments such as outside, in the dark, or with sunglasses. Face ID uses depth sensors to scan your face and even if you have a mask or glasses on, it will detect your face and not let anyone else use your phone. Once you set up Face ID, you will still be asked to enter a passcode while setting up an iPhone

13 because of past cases where people's faces were not enrolled properly but should be able to unlock their phones just by trying again on their own.

What's New in Version 13?

The best-selling phone just got better! In this latest update, Apple has focused on improving an already near-perfect phone. The iPhone 13 is equipped with the latest and greatest technology available—Wi-Fi, 4G LTE, and Touch ID. It's also thinner, brighter, and faster than ever!

What About the Screen?

The screen on the iPhone 13 is a 5.8-inch display, which means it fits into a smaller footprint than previous models. The reduced size makes the phone easier to hold and use in one hand. However, it also maintains iOS' signature aesthetics.

What About the Speed?

How fast is this thing? the speed is faster without compromising its signature look. The iPhone 13 is blisteringly fast! It features a new A12 Bionic chipset, which has been optimized to run at even higher speeds without burning through battery life.

Chapter 1.

Introduction and Terminology

The iPhone 13 Features

The iPhone 13 designs are identical to the iPhone 12, which features flat edges, a durable glass back, and a Ceramic Shield display upfront. The update also included MagSafe charging and 5G.

This time around, it is slightly thicker and comes in a series of new colors: pink, blue, starlight (silver and gold mix), midnight (black), and red. The battery life is longer by an hour or more when in regular use, and we have the new A15 Bionic processor that helps improve photo processing. The iPhone 13 Pro and Pro Max are designed for detailed-minded users. They arrive with a stainless steel frame and a 3 lens-camera system with upgraded Wide, Ultra-Wide, and Telephoto lenses that offer sophisticated photography options. These phones also come with an adaptive refresh up to 120HZ, one feature it doesn't share with other iPhone 13 models.

Sizes

The iPhone 13 is 5.78 inches tall, 2.82 inches wide, and 0.30 inches thick.

The iPhone 13 mini is 5.18 inches tall, 2.53 inches wide, and 0.30 inches thick at 4.97 ounces (141 grams).

The iPhone 13 Pro is 5.8 x 2.8 x 0.3 inches, while the Pro Max is 6.3 x 3.1 x 0.3 inches.

The mini is the lightest phone in the iPhone 13 lineup and next to it is the iPhone 13 at 6.14 ounces (174 grams).

iPhone 13 Pro weighs 7.2 ounces and the Pro Max, 8.5 ounces.

Like its predecessor, the screen size for iPhone 13 Pro is 6.1 inches and 6.7 inches for Pro Max, compared to just a 5.4-inch screen for iPhone 13 mini.

Design

The iPhone 13 still looks the same: the same flat edges on all the iPhone 13 lineup, as well as the same body design.

However:

- Notch is smaller by about 20%.
- Rear cameras are placed diagonally instead of the previous vertical arrangement.
- The button placement is slightly different.

The smaller notch on the front display is where the True Depth Camera, microphone, and speaker are housed. It offers more content viewing space.

There are antenna bands at the top of the phone and the side as well. You'll also find the power button on the right, and on the left is the Volume/Silence buttons. All the models have microphones and speaker holes at the bottom. Also, there is a lightning port for charging. On the left side is the SIM slot. The back of the iPhone 13 model is a square camera bump with a new diagonal lens arrangement that gives room for the camera's new sensor-shift optical image stabilization.

Display

All phones use Apple's Ceramic Shield cover glass for drop protection. A flexible OLED Super Retina XDR display extends right into the chassis of all the iPhone 13 models.

The resolution for iPhone 13 is 2532 x1170 with 460 pixels per inch. Its Pro Max model is 2778 x 1284. For mini, it is 2340 x1080 resolution with 476 pixels per inch.

Their Super Retina XDR Displays provide 28% more brightness. For HDR, you get 1200 nits max brightness with True Tone, Wide Color, and Haptic Touch. True Tone matches the display's color temperature to the ambient lighting. Wide Color offers rich, true-to-life hues, and Haptic Touch provides feedback; the standard max brightness is 800 nits but for iPhone 13 Pro the standard max is 1000 nits.

Storage Space

Storage starts with 128GB on all iPhone 13 models. iPhone 13 and iPhone 13 mini have up to 512GB of storage space. The iPhone 13 Pro models, on the other hand, can have a maximum storage space of 1TB.

Water Resistance

The iPhone 13 and 13 mini have an IP68 water-resistant rating. They can withstand a depth of up to 6 meters (19.7 feet) for up to 30 minutes, just like the iPhone 12 models. The 6 in the IP68 number pertains to dust resistance, so the iPhone 13 can hold up to dirt and dust. It is the highest dust resistance rating ever. The 8 in the number refers to water resistance, giving the iPhone 13 the capacity to withstand splashes, rain, and accidental water exposure. Nevertheless, protect your phones from liquid exposure as the warranty does not cover damages caused by this.

RAM

The iPhone 13 models have 4GB RAM. The iPhone 13 Pro models have 6 RAM, just like the iPhone 12 models.

Color Range

Pink, blue, midnight (black), starlight white, and red are all available in iPhone 13 colors, which has been true this year for the non-Pro models.

Chapter 2. The Most Important Things to Know

Rather than cramming everything into a big screen, Apple is sticking to its tried and tested formula for design and functionality. This means that the iPhone 13 isn't a radical departure from the iPhone 12. If you're a regular user, you'll probably see very little difference between the two. One of the noticeable differences is that the new iPhone has a much thicker bezel. The screen still uses the same size bezels as before, and you can't really tell the difference.

The infamous notch that houses Face ID, the front-facing camera and the earpiece on the iPhone 13 all have been reduced by 20 percent. Since it was initially introduced on the iPhone X in 2017, the notch has changed for the first time. This change will increase the screen real domain along the phone's top edge.

The iPhone 13 looks nearly identical to its predecessors, which means there aren't any major changes outside of upgraded specs. Nowadays, every smartphone maker uses similar body styles, so the fact that Apple is stuck with the same basic form factor is actually refreshing after years of seeing more radical redesigns.

However, the iPhone 13 brings a few noteworthy updates under the hood. For starters, both the iPhone 13 and iPhone 13 Pro gain support for Gigabit LTE speeds via AT&T's recently acquired network infrastructure provider, Nokia Networks. This should make browsing the web much less sluggish than before thanks to improved data transfer rates. In addition, the iPhone 13 gains Bluetooth 5.2 capabilities, allowing devices to connect at up to twice the speed of previous models.

As expected, all three models of the iPhone 13 come equipped with Face ID authentication technology. And unlike last year's iPhone 11 models, they now include dual rear cameras instead of just one. These twin lenses offer optical zoom, slow-motion video recording, and portrait mode for taking great selfies.

The iPhone 13 Pro brings even more photography power to bear compared to older models. It includes four different lens options— including a telephoto lens capable of capturing ultra-wide-angle shots and a wide-angle lens that captures images with almost no distortion. There's also a low light mode that allows users to capture clear photos in dark environments.

All three models also sport wireless charging capabilities, though the iPhone 13 Pro has the largest battery capacity out of the bunch. Apple says that it can charge the device completely within 30 minutes using the Qi standard, which makes it the fastest way to top off your phone.

If you want to use the iPhone 13 to watch movies on the go, you'll need to purchase Apple TV+ through iTunes. But if you already own a subscription or purchased Apple TV+, then you can download the app on the iPhone directly and start watching content right away. You can also buy individual episodes for $4.99 each. And because the iPhone 13 series supports Apple Arcade, you can play new games without spending money on in-app purchases.

The iOS

FaceTime can now view videos and share content with others; there is a new Focus mode for managing notifications; and Maps, Messages, Wallet, Weather, and other built-in apps are among the top iOS 15 features.

Display

Like last year, the iPhone 13 is available in a 6.1-inch screen size, and it features Super Retina XDR OLED technology. The non-Pro models, Apple claims, can deliver a brightness of up to 800 nits.

Camera

For the iPhone 13, Apple has updated its camera to feature a new 12MP ultra-wide sensor that allows for 47% more light to enter the circuit. This sensor-shift optical image stabilization feature, which was previously available only on the iPhone 12 Pro Max, allows the 12MP main wide-angle camera on the iPhone 13 to capture beautiful photos in many lighting conditions. With the new iPhone 13, you'll also get Photographic Styles, which in real-time render your photos based on your personal preferences. This is much more than a filter; it applies the right adjustments to different scenes to get the best photos. Cinematic Mode offers you high-end cinematography with Dolby Vision HDR for iPhone 13. Cinematic Mode's claim to fame is its ability to shift focus and also follow the subject of your video. The focus shifts from where the subject is looking to where the subject is looking if the subject moves. If the person turns away, the focus shifts to where the subject is looking.

Apple says that the upgraded camera hardware will help improve photo quality across its entire lineup, not just the iPhone 13. The company has been working hard to update its imaging software as well, and today it announced several enhancements aimed at improving still image and video shooting performance.

For example, the iPhone 13 Pro and Pro Max gain support for the RAW file format. RAW files contain the full-color depth of an original print, and since the process converts the sensor data into an uncompressed digital signal, you can take advantage of the extra detail.

You can also choose to shoot videos with H.265 compression instead of the usual HEVC (H.265) codec. This lets you save storage space while preserving the highest possible video resolution.

A15 Bionic Processor

The A15 Bionic system-on-chip, which is Apple's most advanced chip ever, is included in the iPhone 13 and is based on a 5nm process with six cores. The iPhone 13 has powerful machine learning capabilities, including iOS 15's new Live Text feature and Siri's on-device speech recognition, because of enhancements to the Neural Engine. The iPhone 13's quad-core GPU is perfect for graphically demanding gaming and photography, with Apple claiming it is 30% faster than that on an Android phone.

Battery

This year, Apple has fitted an updated battery to the iPhone 13, meaning it will last two and a half hours longer than the iPhone 12. The iPhone 13 can now charge with 20W wired and 15W wireless charging via MagSafe.

Final Verdict on the New Features

The iPhone 13's most notable upgrades are its cameras and the A15 Bionic chip. The notch has been reduced, and the iPhone 13's photography capabilities are certainly impressive. This phone has a lot to offer over its predecessor. The iPhone 13 gets sensor-shift stabilization, and ultra-wide improvements across the board are equally impressive, without forgetting battery life improvements.

Chapter 3.
Let's Start With Your iPhone

Set Up and Get Started

Setting up a new iPhone is pretty easy, but even after a couple of years with an iPhone, it's important to continue to keep things updated. It's important to keep your device up to date and keep your security software updated. So if you're upgrading, it's important to know the steps to get set up.

Step 1: Connect Your iPhone

You'll need a free Apple ID, but you can set one up easily in just a couple of minutes. First, you'll need to go to the Apple store or connect with an Apple store online. Once you've got your free Apple ID, you'll be able to create and set up iCloud Backup on your phone to back up and restore your device.

Step 2: Set Up iCloud Backup

Once you're in the store, go to "Manage your Apple ID." Once there, you'll go to Backup and restore, and click on "Backup and restore." Ensure you are using the latest version of iOS that's available.

Make sure you're connected to your Apple ID and then choose the option that says "Manually restore with this computer" and plug in your iPhone.

Step 3: Set Up iCloud Backup on Your iPhone

After you've finished setting up iCloud, you'll set up iCloud backups on your iPhone. With an iCloud backup, you'll have the ability to quickly restore your iPhone if you lose it or break it or change it. To set up iCloud backups, go to Settings>iCloud>iCloud Backup.

You'll have to set up iCloud backups to take place daily and make sure to select the iCloud option when prompted.

It's important to make sure you're connected to Wi-Fi when taking iCloud backups on your iPhone, as your mobile data bill will skyrocket.

Step 4: Set Up Passbook

With the iCloud backups ready, we'll be taking a look at how to back up our Passbook as well. With Passbook, you'll be able to set up and share coupons for discounts, have quick access to payment information and even sync with your bank account. If you want to do that, go to Settings>Passbook.

Step 5: Manage Your Apple ID

If you ever wanted to manage your Apple ID, this is the time. The Apple ID is what you use when you want to get a discount with the company and buy the latest products from Apple. You can also change your password, add, remove and even enable iCloud from the Apple ID.

Step 6: Manage Photos

Manage your photos will be easy with your photos and videos, be it in the Camera Roll, Shared Photo Streams, Moments, Live Photos, iTunes Match, or your iCloud Photo Library. You'll be able to manage them from the Photos app.

Step 7: Manage iWork

Manage your iWork documents from within your iWork apps from your Mac, as well as your iPhone. You can also make a switch from one to the other depending on which one you use most, which will make things easy. You can also set a backup of your iWork for a future date if you need to.

Step 8: Manage App Store Purchases

Manage your App Store purchases from within your App Store, as well as from within the Mac. You can also view details on every app that you have purchased and can set them to buy again if you feel that you have overpaid for it. You can also see your last download of apps.

Step 9: Manage iCloud

Manage your iCloud storage within your Mac or your iCloud. You can also set up storage space within your computer's settings. You can buy extra storage space, which is pretty cheap considering how much storage you are getting.

If you have other iCloud storage devices, such as your iPhone, you can access them as well.

Step 10: Manage iCloud Backup

You can set up a backup on your iCloud storage as well as on your iPhone and iPad. You will have to have an internet connection in order to do that, and you'll have to sign in to your iCloud account and select what you want to back up. You can also back up over Wi-Fi to your computer so that you won't have to connect to the internet to back up.

Step 11: Manage Documents and Data

You can view your document storage and data from within your Mac or iCloud. You can also back up your document storage and data.

As mentioned, you can back up your documents and data to your iCloud or from your Mac.

How to Set Up Cellular Service

With new iPhones coming out almost yearly, it can be hard to keep up with new features, but if you're new to the iPhone, there are a few features you'll want to understand to get the most out of the device. One of these is Cellular Service, but first, it's best to explain what it is and how it works.

The truth is, most of the time when you go to purchase an iPhone or even a new phone, you don't buy it with Cellular Service. It's usually an add-on. If you have an iPhone that you bought without cellular service, you can still use it with Cellular Service.

Even though it's an add-on, if you want to add Cellular Service to your iPhone, you still need to make sure you set it up correctly to maximize the functionality of the device and keep you safe and happy with your phone. The iPhone is one of the best phones on the market, but it's not perfect. If you use your iPhone and a Bluetooth speaker and your device is not using the cellular signal, you won't know how to communicate with it.

Apple has brought many upgrades to the iPhone 13 and so it is worth taking a look at how to set up Cellular Service on the device. Below are the best settings to configure on your iPhone 13 to achieve optimal connectivity.

How to Connect Your Phone to a Wi-Fi Network on iPhone 13

1. Go to the iPhone's network menu and go to Wi-Fi.

2. Select the desired Wi-Fi network. At this point, you will be asked to sign in with your Apple ID. You can also add a password in this step.

3. The iPhone 13 offers a few different ways to connect to a Wi-Fi network:

   - If you don't use your phone for too long on a day, the iPhone will automatically connect to a Wi-Fi network if it's nearby.

   - If you have set up an iCloud hotspot and you use the iPhone to connect to your home Wi-Fi network, the phone will automatically connect to it.

   - If you are using a public Wi-Fi network, you can tap on the name of the Wi-Fi network to easily switch to it.

How to Set Up Cellular Service

1. Open the Settings app. Go to General> Network. You should see the list of connections on the network.

2. If you don't, it is possible to reset it. Go to General> Reset> Reset Network Settings. You can do this after your cellular service has been set up. It's probably a good idea to do this now. This step could wipe your data.

3. Scroll down until you find Mobile Network. Tap on it.

4. Tap on the slider to turn off or on Cellular Data.

5. In the upper part of the screen, you should see a bar with the signal strength. It should say "no service" if you're having a hard time seeing the signal bars or you should see bars if

you're having a hard time seeing the signal bars. Tap on the slider to turn off or on cellular data.

6. If you're seeing bars, tap on More. It should show "Cellular data is connected.

7. Tap on "Use for cellular data only."

8. If you turn on cellular data, you can get the signal bars.

9. When you use cellular data, you should see the bar get bigger and bigger as you use the cellular data. If you don't see the bars, do a factory reset. If you are using cellular data, you will see the bar get bigger and bigger as you use cellular data.

10. If you have a cellular data problem, follow the steps listed above. If the cellular data bars don't show up, turn off cellular data by going to Network in the Settings app, then go to Cellular Data.

How to Check Data Usage and Battery Levels

You can check your cellular data usage as well as the battery percentage on the phone. You will also receive a notification letting you know if the battery is low and needs to be charged.

The settings are located under cellular and it's pretty much self-explanatory.

How to Enable/Disable Your Device

You can also see the current device status, such as enable/disable or turn on/off the device. These options are located under cellular settings.

How to Turn on the Location Services

You can activate or disable the device's location services under cellular settings.

How to Enable/Disable the Mobile Data/Wi-Fi Hotspot

You can switch on or off the phone's mobile data or Wi-Fi hotspot features. These options are located under cellular settings.

How to Activate or Deactivate iCloud Data

You can activate or deactivate the new carrier's cellular data plans, in case the new carrier's sim card is connected to the phone. To activate or deactivate the data, you'll need to go to iCloud. You can find more details about iCloud under iCloud settings. This is only a shortlist of the cellular settings options.

You will need to follow similar steps to switch carriers on your iPhone.

Chapter 4.
Let's Start With the Basics Together

Wake iPhone

The iPhone turns off the screen to save power, locks it for safety, and sleeps when you are not making use of it. You can wake up and open it quickly when you want to use your iPhone again.

To wake your device, do any of the below:

- Press the side button.

IPHONE 13 USER GUIDE

- Raise your device.

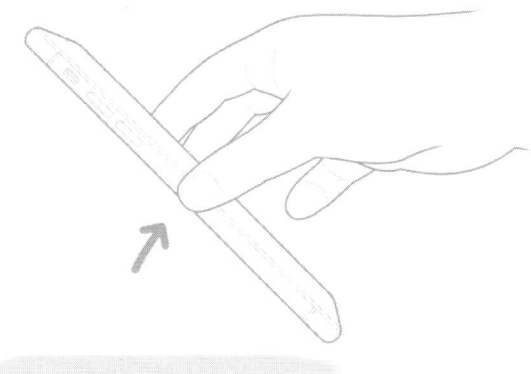

- Touch the screen.

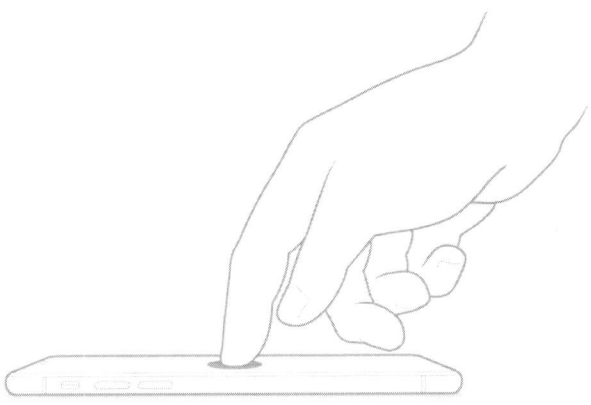

Open Your Device Using Face ID

If you set up Face ID while setting up your phone, you can use it to open your phone.

1. Touch the display or lift your device to wake it up, then look at the iPhone.

2. The lock icon animates from locked to unlocked to show that your device is opened.

3. Swipe up from the bottom edge of your display.

Open Your iPhone With the Login Code

1. Swipe up from the lower part of your lock screen.
2. Type the passcode.

Unlock Your iPhone With Your Apple Watch

First, you need to pair your Apple Watch with your iPhone, to do this simply launch the Apple Watch application on your iPhone, then adhere to the directives on your screen.

To Unlock Your iPhone Using Your Watch

You would need an Apple Watch Series 3 or after running WatchOS 7.4 or after.

1. Launch the Settings application on your iPhone> Face ID & Passcode.
2. Go down, then activate Apple Watch (under Unlock using Apple Watch).

If you own more than a watch, activate the setting for all of them.

When you wear an Apple Watch and face mask, lift the iPhone or touch it, then look at your device.

To open your iPhone, your smartwatch should have a passcode, must be open and in your hand, and close to your iPhone.

Insert a Nano SiM

1. Insert the SIM ejector into the small slot of the SIM card holder, and then press it on the iPhone to eject the holder.

IPHONE 13 USER GUIDE

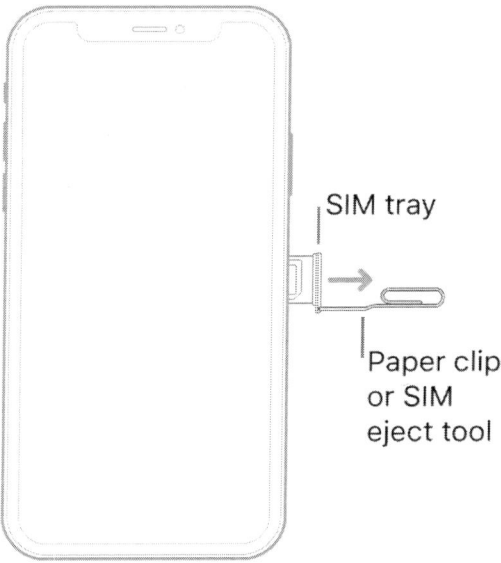

2. Take out the plate from your Phone.

3. Put the SIM in the tray. The right angle determines the true direction.

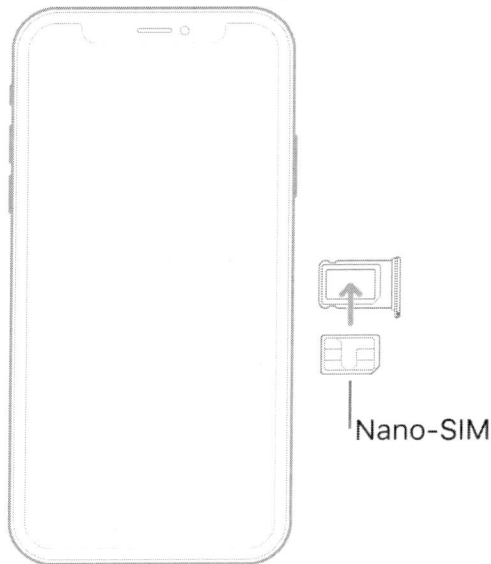

4. Put the tray back on the device.

5. If you have already set a PIN on the nano-SIM, enter the PIN correctly when prompted.

Basic Gestures

Manage your iPhone and its apps with a few basic gestures:

- **Touch:** Gently tap using one finger.

- **Long touch:** Touch and hold elements in an application or the Control Center to get a preview of contents and perform some quick actions.

- **Swipe:** Quickly move a finger across your display.

- **Scroll:** Move a finger across the display without raising it.

- **Zoom:** Put 2 fingers on your display close to each other. Spread the fingers apart to zoom in, or bring them close to each other to zoom out.

  You can also tap a picture or web page two times to zoom in, and tap it twice again to zoom out.

- **Go to the Home Screen:** Swipe up from the lower part of your display.

- **Fast access to controls:** Swipe down from the upper right part of your display to launch the control center. Enter the Settings application> Control Centre to add or remove controls.

- **Launch the application switcher:** Swipe up from the bottom of your display, stop at the middle of your display then raise your finger. Swipe right to view all open applications and then touch the application you want to use.

- **Take a screenshot:** Press the volume up and side button simultaneously.

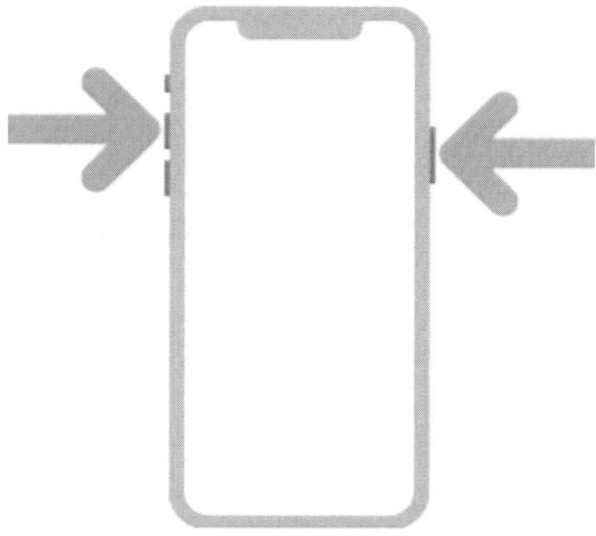

- **Use Apple Pay:** Press the side button twice to show your default card then look at your device to confirm with Face ID.

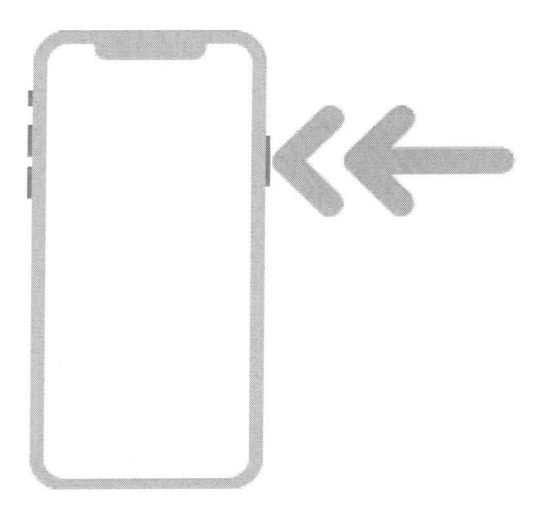

- **Switch off:** hold down the side and any of the volume buttons simultaneously till the slider shows up, and then pull the top slide to power off. Or enter the settings application> General> Shut Down.

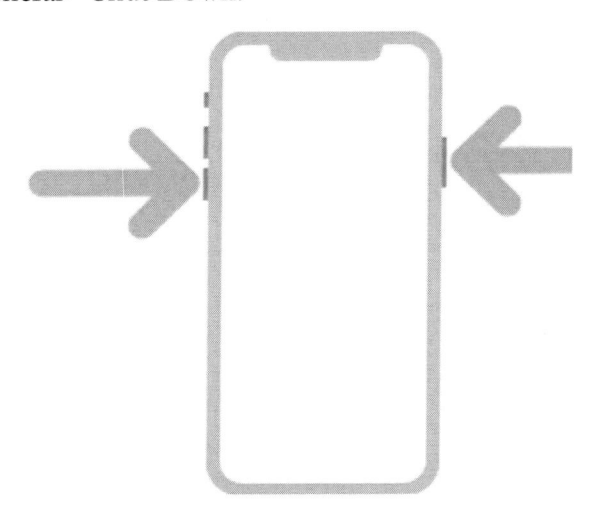

Put Your Device In Silent Mode

You can put your device in silent mode by flipping the switch at the side of your device. You can disable silent mode by flipping the switch once more.

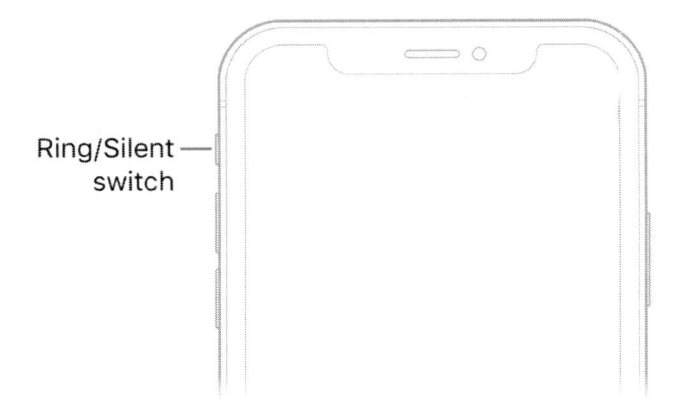

Ring/Silent switch

When silent mode is deactivated, the iPhone plays all sounds. When the silent mode is activated, the iPhone will not sound or play warnings or other sound effects (but the iPhone may still vibrate).

Launch Applications on Your Device

You can quickly launch applications from your Home Screen or the application library.

- Swipe up from the lower part of your display to go to the home screen.

IPHONE 13 USER GUIDE

- Swipe to view more applications.

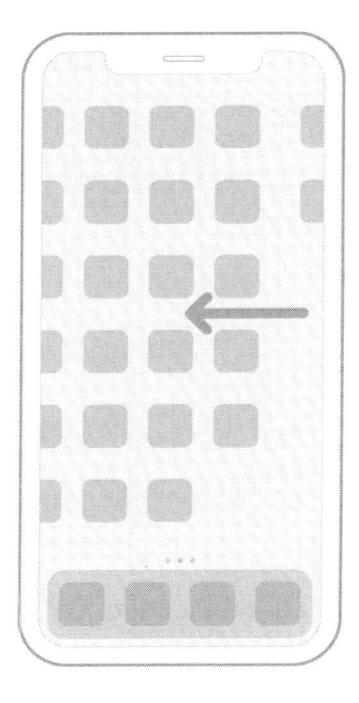

- Browse through every page in your home screen to display the Application Library, where applications are in order by category.

- Touch an icon to launch an application.

- To go back to the app library, swipe up from the lower part of your display.

Remove Applications From Your Device

You can remove applications from iPhone easily. Do any of the below:

- **Remove an application from the Home screen:** hold down the application on your Home screen, touch Remove application, then touch the Remove app from the Home screen button to leave it in the application library, or touch Delete application to uninstall the application from your device.

- **Uninstall an application from the application library and the Home screen:** hold down an application in the application library, touch Delete Application, then touch delete

Find Settings on Your Device

In the settings application, you can change the iPhone settings, like the password, notification sounds, etc.

- Touch the settings application.

Tap Settings to change your iPhone settings (volume, screen brightness, and more).

- Type on a term in the search to display the settings (if available).

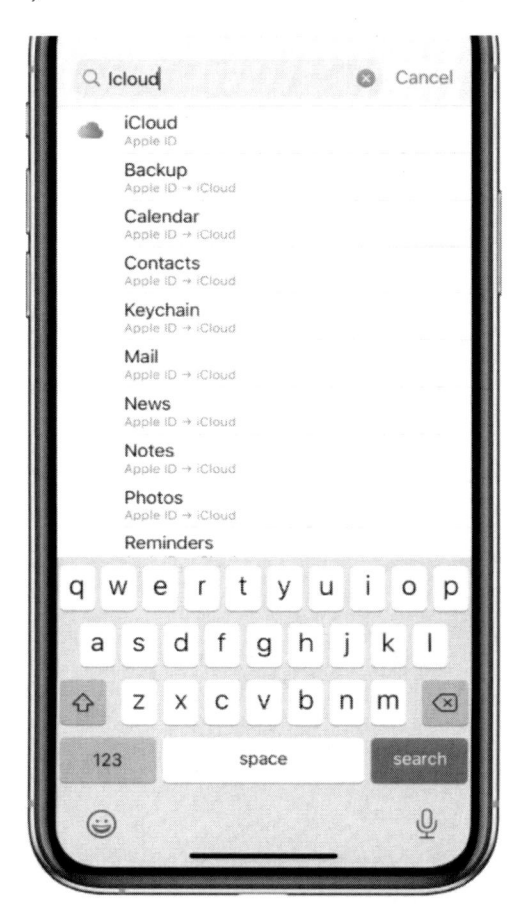

Use and Personalize the Control Centre

Your device Controls Centre gives you quick access to handy controls, including flight mode, Focus, volume, display brightness and applications.

To launch the Control Center, simply swipe down from the upper right part of your display. Swipe up to conceal the control center.

To Access More Controls in the Control Center

Most controls have extra options. Hold down the controls to see the options. For instance, in the Control Center you can do any of the below:

Touch and hold to see Camera options.

- Hold down the control panel on the left, and touch the AirDrop button ⓐ to launch the AirDrop preferences.

- Hold down the Camera icon 🗖 to take a selfie, take a picture, etc.

To Add and Arrange Controls

You can personalize your controls center by adding more controls and shortcuts to applications, like Notes voice memos, etc.

- Head over to the Setting application> Control Center.
- • Touch the Add ⊕ or Remove ⊖ Controls icon.
- • To adjust the control, tap on the Mode button ≡ beside a control, and then drag it to a new location.

Disable Access to the Controls Center in Applications

Enter the Settings application> Control Centre and disable Access within applications.

Connect to and Disconnect From a WiFi Network

In the control center, touch the Wi-Fi switch button 🛜 to connect; press again to disconnect.

To view the name of the connected Wi-Fi network, hold down the Wi-Fi Switch button 🛜.

Set the Date and Time

- Enter the Setting application, touch General> Date and Time.
- Enable any of the below:
    - ✓ Set automatically
    - ✓ 24-hour time

Change the Sounds and Vibration

Change the iPhone sound when you receive a call, text, e-mail, reminder, etc.

You can feel a tap known as haptic feedback after performing certain actions, like when you hold down the Camera icon on the Home Screen.

- Enter the Settings application> Sounds and Haptics.
- Drag the slider under Ringers and Alerts to determine the volume for every sound.
- To determine the vibration & sound, touch a sound type, like ringtone or text tone.
- Do any of the below:
  - ✓ Select a tone (scroll to see all).
  - ✓ Touch Vibration, then select a vibration style or touch Create New Vibration to create yourself.

Activate or Deactivate Haptic Feedback

- Enter the Settings application> Sounds and Haptics.
- Activate or deactivate System Haptics.

When System Haptics is deactivated, you will not hear or feel the vibration from incoming calls and notifications.

Set Your Language & Region on Your Device

- Enter the Setting application> General> Languages and regions.
- Set the below:
  - ✓ Language for iPhone
  - ✓ Region
  - ✓ Calendar format
  - ✓ Temperature unit

- To add a different language & keyboards to your device, touch the Add Language button and then choose a language.

Rename Your iPhone

You can change the name of your device that is used by Personal Hotspot, AirDrop, iCloud, and by your PC.

- Enter the Settings application, touch General, tap on About, and click on Name.
- Touch ⊗, type another name and then touch Done.

Change Your Wallpaper

On your device, select a photo or image as the wallpaper for your device Lock or Home screen.

- Enter the Settings application> Wallpapers> Select New Wallpaper.
- Do any of the below:
  - ✓ Select a preset image in the group at the upper part of your display.
  - ✓ Choose one of your pictures (touch an album, then touch a photo).
  - ✓ Click the Parallax Effect button to activate Perspective Zoom.
- Touch Set, then select one the below:
  - ✓ Set lock screen
  - ✓ Set home screen
  - ✓ Both

Use a Live Picture as Your Wallpaper

- Enter the Setting application> Wallpapers> select New Wallpaper.
- Do any of the below:
  - ✓ Touch Live, then select a live picture.
  - ✓ Touch your Live Photo folder, then select a Live Picture.
- Touch Set, then select Set Lock Screen or Both.
- Long-touch the Lock Screen to play your Live Picture.

Use the Display Zoom to Magnify the iPhone Display

You can find larger screen controls with Zoom Display.

- Enter the Settings application> Display and Brightness.
- Touch the View button (under Display Zoom).
- Select Zoomed, and then touch Set.

Activate or Deactivate Dark Mode

The Dark Mode gives your device a Dark color scheme that is great for low light conditions. When the dark mode is active, you can use your iPhone without worrying about the person next to you for example, when you are reading in bed, you do not have to worry about disturbing the person beside you.

Do any of the below:

- Launch the Control Center, hold down the Brightness button ☀, and touch the Appearance button ◐ to activate or deactivate Dark Mode.
- Enter the Settings application> Display and brightness, then choose Dark to activate dark mode, or choose light to deactivate it.

Schedule Dark Mode to Activate & Deactivate Automatically

- Enter the Setting application> Display and Brightness.
- Enable Automatic, then touch Options.
- Choose between Custom and Sunset to Sunrise.

If you select Custom, touch the option to set when you want to activate or deactivate Dark Mode.

If you choose Sunrise to Sunrise, the iPhone makes use of the information from your clock and geolocation to determine when the night will be for you.

Adjust the Screen Brightness Manually

To reduce or increase the iPhone screen brightness, do any of the below:

- Launch the control center and then pull the brightness button.

- Enter the Settings application> Display and Brightness, and then drag the slider.

Automatically Adjust the Brightness of the Screen

- Enter the Setting application> Accessibility.
- Touch Display and Text Size, then activate Auto-Brightness.

Enable or Disable True Tone

Enable True Tone to automatically adapt the color& intensity of your screen to fit the light around you.

Do any of the below:

- Open the Control Center, hold down the brightness button, then touch the Light Tone button, to activate or deactivate True Tone.

- Enter the setting application> Display & Brightness, then enable or disable True Tone.

Activate or Deactivate Night Shift

You can enable Night Shift, which is useful when you are in a dark room during the day.

Open the control center, hold down the brightness button ☀, and press the Night Shift button ☾.

Access Features From Your Device Lock Screen

The Lock Screen, which displays the date & time and your latest notifications, shows when you switch on or wake up your device. Even when the iPhone is locked, you can access useful features and info from the Lock Screen. From the lock screen, do any of the below:

- Launch the camera: swipe left. You can hold down the Camera icon 📷, and then raise your finger.

- Launch the control center

- See previous message: swipe up from the middle of your display

- See Today's view: swipe to the right

Take a Screenshot

You can capture your display and share it with others or save it on your device.

- Press & release the side & volume up button simultaneously.

- Touch the screenshot in the bottom-left part of your display, and touch Done.

- Choose Save to Files, or Photos, or delete the screenshot.

If you decide to store it in Photos, you can view them in the Screenshots folder in the Photos application or in the All Photos folder if you turn on iCloud Photos in the settings> Photo.

Capture a Full-Page Screenshot

You can get a full-page, scrolling screenshot of a web page, document, or e-mail that is longer than your device's display length. Screenshots are saved in PDF format.

- Press and release the side & volume up button at the same time.
- Touch the screenshot in the bottom left part, and then touch Full Page.
- Do any of the below:
    ✓ Store the image on your device: Touch Done, select Save PDF to Files, select a location, and touch the Save button.
    ✓ Share the image: Touch the Share button, select a way to share (for example, AirDrop, Messages, or Mail), enter other desired information, and send PDF.

Record Your iPhone Screen

- Enter the Setting application> Control Centre, and touch the add button beside screen-recording.
- Open the control center, touch the record button, and then wait for 3 secs before your device starts to record its screen.
- To end the recording, launch the Control Center, touch the End record icon or the red status bar at the upper part of your display, and touch stop.
- Open the Photo application, then open what you recorded.

Change or Lock the Screen Orientation

Most applications look different when you rotate your device.

You can lock the orientation of your display so that it does not change when the iPhone is rotated.

Launch the Control Centre and touch the Lock button ⊖.

When you lock the display orientation, the Orientation Lock icon ⊖ shows up on the status bar.

Arrange Applications in Folders

You can organize your applications into folders so that they can be easy to look for on your Home Screen.

To Create a Folder

- Hold down any application on your Home screen, and tap Edit Home screen.
- The applications would start jiggling.
- To make a folder, drag an application onto another application.
- Drag other applications into the folder.
- To change the folder name, touch the name box, and type a name.
- When you are done, touch Done.

To delete a folder, touch the folder to launch it, then remove all the applications from it by dragging them out. The folder is automatically erased.

Transfer Applications on Your Home Screen

You can change the appearance of your home screen-move applications around or drag them to another Home Screen page.

- Hold down the application on your home screen, then tap Edit Home Screen.
- The application would start jiggling.
- Drag the application to any of the locations below:
  - ✓ Anywhere on the page
  - ✓ Dock at the lower part of your screen
  - ✓ Another home screen page
  - ✓ Drag the application to the edge of your display. You might need to wait some seconds for the new page to show up. The number of dots on top of the dock indicates how many pages there are and which of them you see.

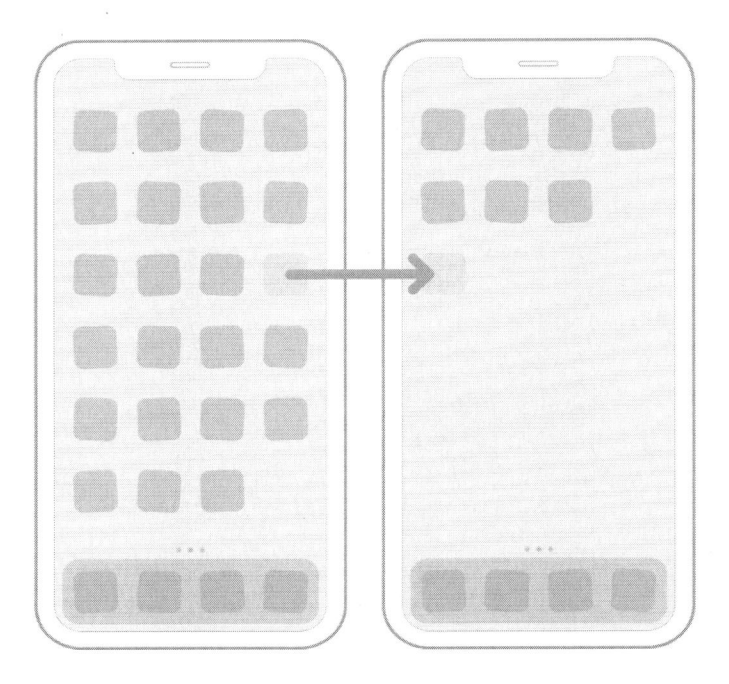

✓ When you're done, touch Done.

Hide and Display the Home Screen Page

You can get all your applications in the Application library, so you might not need a lot of Home Screen pages. You can hide the home screen pages, in others to bring the Application Library closer to the First Hone Screen Page.

- Hold down the Home Screen. The applications would start jiggling.
- Touch the dots at the lower part of your display.

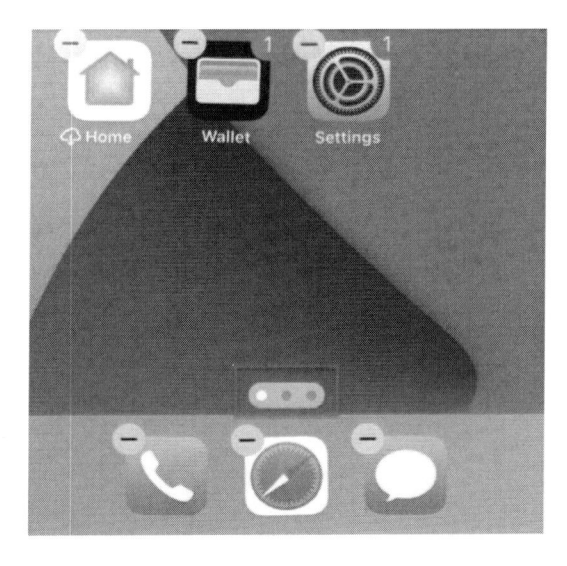

- Touch the checkmarks to conceal a home page.
- Touch the checkmark to display the page again.
- Touch Done two times.

Multitask Using Picture in Picture

You can multitask on your device. For instance, you can make use of another application while making a Face-Time call or watching a video.

When making use of FaceTime or watching a movie, touch the "Picture in Picture" button .

The video window would reduce to a part of your display so that you can view other applications. Do any of the below:

- **Resize video:** To make the video window bigger, pinch open. Pinch close to make it smaller.

- **Display & conceal controls:** Touch the video window.

- **Move the window:** You can move the window by dragging it to another part of your display.

- **Conceal the video window:** You can conceal the window by dragging it to the right or left edge of your display.

- **Close the window:** Touch the Close button .

- **Go back to the full video display:** In the small video window, touch the Full-Screen button .

Dictate Text on Your Device

Rather than typing, you can simply dictate.

- Enter the Settings application> General> Keyboard.

- Activate Enable Dictation.

To Dictate

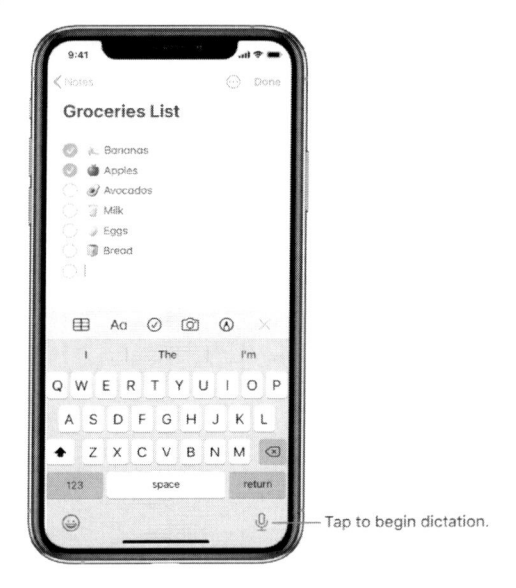

- Touch the Dict icon 🎤 on the on-screen keyboard, and then start talking.

- When you are done touch the Keypad ⌨.

To add punctuation, Say the punctuation mark while dictating, For instance, "Dear Sandra comma the result is on the desk exclamation mark" would become "Dear Sandra, the result is on the desk!"

Select & Edit the Text

You can use the on-screen keyboard to highlight & edit text.

- To select a text, do any of the below:

    ✓ Highlight a word: Touch the word two times with a finger.

    ✓ Highlight a paragraph: Triple-tap using a finger.

    ✓ Highlight a sentence: Double-touch & hold the first word in the sentence, then drag it to the last word.

- Once you have selected the text you want to edit, you can write or touch the option to view the editing options:

    ✓ Cut.

    ✓ Copy.

    ✓ Paste.

    ✓ Change: See the suggested replacement.

    ✓ B/I/U: Format the highlighted text.

    ✓ More display button : See other options.

Store Keystrokes Using Text Replacements

Make text edits that can be used to replace a word or phrase by typing just a few letters. For instance, Type "OMW" to insert On My Way.

To create text replacements, adhere to the directives below:

- As you type in the text box, hold down the Emoji button ☺, or the Switch keypad ⊕.
- Touch Keyboard settings, then touch Text Replacement.
- Touch the Add button +.
- Write the phrase in the phrase box and type the shortcut you want to make use of in the short field.

Add or Change Keyboards on Your iPhone

- Enter the Settings application> General> Keyboard.
- Touch Keyboard, then do any of the below:
  - ✓ Add keyboard: Touch Add a New Keyboard and then select a keyboard from the catalog. Repeat the process to add more keys.

- ✓ Remove a keyboard: Touch the edit button, Touch the minus button ⊖ beside the keyboard you plan on erasing, touch the Delete button, and touch Done.

- ✓ Rearrange your keyboard catalog: Touch the Edit button, drag the Edit button ≡ beside the keyboard to the new location, and touch Done.

Switch to Another Keyboard

- As you type, hold down the Emoji key ☺, or the Switch keypad 🌐.

- Touch the keyboard name you want to move.

You can also press the next keyboard Emoji button ☺ or keyboard keys 🌐 to move from one keyboard to another. Keep tapping to continue moving to another keyboard.

Use Another Keyboard Layout

You can use other keyboard layouts.

- Enter the settings application> General> Keyboard »Keyboard.

- Touch a language at the upper part of your display, then choose another layout from the list.

AirDrop

With AirDrop, you can wirelessly transfer your pictures, videos, web pages, locations, and more to other devices and Macs around you (iOS 7, iPadOS 13, OS X 10.10, or later). AirDrop transmits data via both Wi-Fi & Bluetooth, which you need to Enable. To utilize AirDrop, you need to sign in using an Apple ID. The transmission is locked for security.

To Send Things Via Airdrop

- Open the item, then touch share, 📤, More options icon •••, AirDrop button, or another icon that displays the app's sharing preferences.

- Touch the AirDrop icon 📶 in the share menu, then touch the nearby AirDrop user's profile picture.

If you can't find the person as a close-by AirDrop user, tell them to launch the control center on their device and allow AirDrop to receive things. To send to people using a Mac, tell them to let themselves be found on AirDrop in the Finder.

Allowing Others to Send Stuff to Your Device Via Airdrop

- Launch the control center, hold down the control panel on the left, and then click the AirDrop icon 📶.

- Touch Contact or Everybody to choose those that you can get things from.

Draw in Applications Using Markup

In applications like messaging, mail, notes, and books, you can write in images, screenshots, PDFs, and more using special drawing tools.

Draw Using Markup

- In the compatible application, touch markup or the markup icon ⓐ.

- On the markup toolbar, touch a pen, marker, or pencil tool, and write or draw using your fingers.

- To conceal the markup toolbar, touch the conceal markup button ⊚ or Done

When drawing, do any of the below:

- Change the weight of the line: touch the tool you are using to draw in the toolbar, and select an option.

- Adjust the transparency: touch the tool you are using to draw in the toolbar, and pull the slide.

- Adjust the color: Touch the Color Selector button ● in the toolbar, and then select a color.

- Undo Error: Click the Revert button ↺.

- Draw a straight line: touch the ruler in the toolbar, then draw a line along the ruler's edge.

  ✓ To change the ruler's angle, hold down the ruler using 2 fingers, then rotate your fingers.

  ✓ You can change the ruler's location by dragging it with a finger.

  ✓ Touch the ruler tool once more to hide it.

To Erase an Error

Use the Eraser tool to clear an error

- Erase using the pixel Eraser: remove the error with your finger.

- Erase using the object cleaner: tap the object.

- Change between the object and pixel eraser: touch the eraser tool once more and select one of the Erasers.

Perform Quick Actions From the Home Screen & the Application Library

Hold down applications to enter the fast action menu on the Application Library & the Home Screen.

For instance:

- Hold down the camera icon 📷, then select Take Selfie.
- Hold down the Maps icon, then select send my location.
- Hold down the note app icon 📝, and select New note.

Note: If you hold down an application for a long time before selecting an action, all of the applications would start jiggling. Touch Done and try again.

Live Text

While viewing a picture in the Photo application ●, you can utilize the Live Text feature to copy and share text in the picture, translate language, open a site or make calls.

To use Live Text, open a picture, then do any of the below:

- Highlight the text in the picture: touch the live button ⊡ to highlight the text.

- Copy the text: hold down a word, select what you want and touch copy. To select everything touch, select all.

- Search for articles on the Internet: long-touch a word, select what you want, then touch Look Up.

- Translate text: long-touch a word, highlight what you want, and then click the Translate button.

- Share text: long-touch a word, select what you want, touch share, and choose what you want to share.

Visual Look Up

Get more information about famous places, art, plants, flowers, pets, and everything else that appears in your pictures (United States only).

- Open an image in full screen; The Visual Look Up button ⓘ shows that there is Visual Look Up information for that image.

- Swipe up on the picture or touch the Visual Look Up button ⓘ.

- Touch the icon that shows up on the picture or on top of the Picture Info window to check out Siri's knowledge and more info about the object.

Set an Alarm

In the Clock application, you can set an alarm on your Phone.

- Tap on Alarm, and touch the Add icon +.

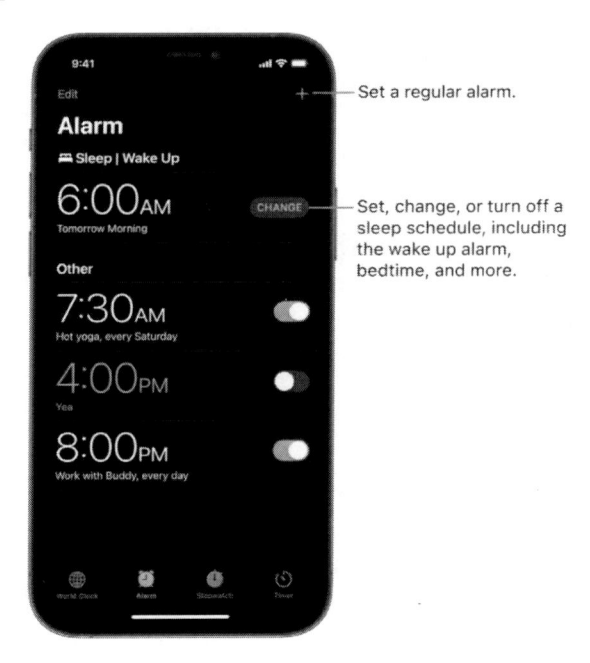

- Set time, and then pick one of the options below:
    - ✓ Repeat: Select the day of the week.
    - ✓ Label: Name the warning something like "Water the crops."
    - ✓ Sound: Select a ringtone, song, or vibration.
    - ✓ Snooze: Give yourself a few minutes of sleep.
- Touch the Save button.

To edit the alarm, click the Edit button on the left, and touch the alarm time.

To turn off an alarm, simply touch the Switch beside the alarm time.

Use the Compass on Your Device

The compass application shows you the direction your device is pointing to, your location, and your altitude.

The bearings, coordinates, and altitude of your device are displayed at the lower part of your display.

Click the coordinates at the lower part of your display to show your location in the maps application.

Automatically Update iPhone

If you did not activate automatic updates when you setting up your device, do this:

- Enter the Settings application> General> Software Updates> Automatic Update.

- Activate Download iOS update and install the iOS update.

When there is an update, the iPhone downloads the update overnight when it is charged and connects to Wi-Fi.

Upgrade Your iPhone Manually

You can check for and install software updates at any time.

- Enter the Setting application> General> Software Update.

Your display would show the current version of iOS on your device and if there is an update.

Measure Someone's Height

You can measure someone's height with your iPhone in the Measure application

- Place your device in a way that the individual you plan on measuring shows on your display from head to toe.

After a while, a line would show on top of the individual's head, and the measurement would be displayed on top of the line.

- Touch ○ to capture a picture.
- To save the image, touch the picture in the bottom left part, touch Done, and select Save to Photo or Files.

Use Your Device Like a Scale

In the measure application, you can utilize your device to see if the object close to you is flat straight, or level.

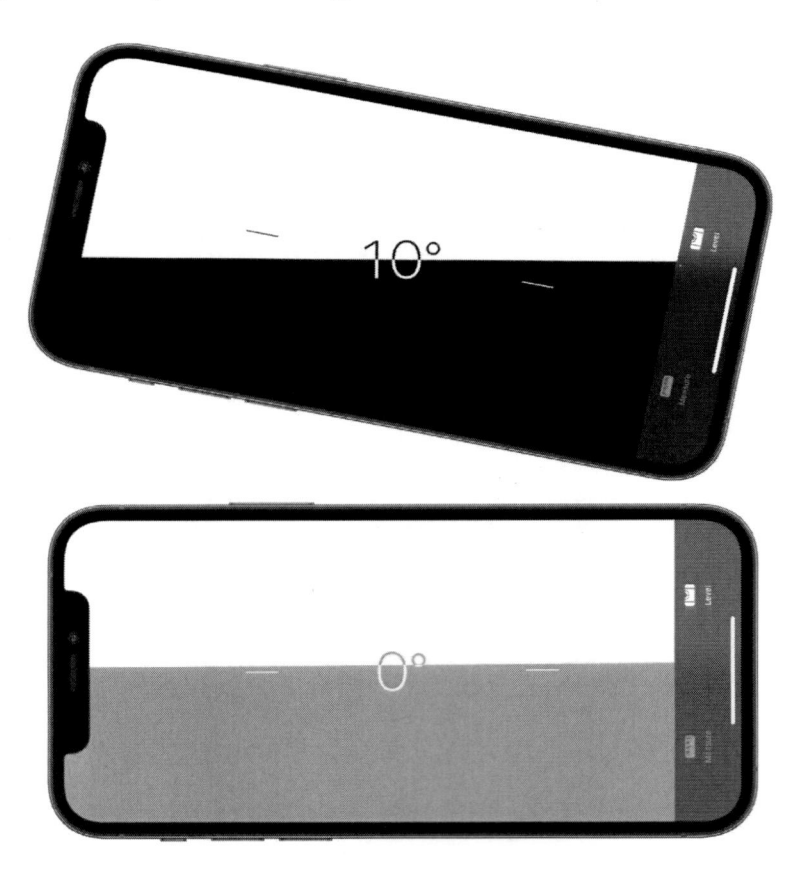

- Open measure.
- Touch Level, and hold your device against the object, like a photo frame.
    - ✓ Adjust the object level: move the object till your iPhone display shows green.
    - ✓ Adjust the curve: touch your display to snap the slope of the first object. Hold your Phone firmly against the other object & move the object till your display shows green.
- Touch your display to reset the level.

Chapter 5.

Apps and App Store

Explore the App Store

The App Store contains all apps compatible with the device and makes it easy to find, buy, and install. The apps available for download in the store have been reviewed by Apple and deemed safe and suitable for use.

To locate apps, click on the App Store and type in word(s) relating to the app in the top-left-hand corner of the Apps Store window and then press Enter. A list of apps will be populated on the screen. You can then click on the app's name or icon to see the description, supported languages, file size, previews, ratings, compatibility with Apple devices, and view existing user ratings and reviews.

Download and Purchase Apps

To download a particular app, tap on the button that displays the price or "Get" and then click on the button one more time to buy the app or install it (if the app is free). To purchase an app or in-app content, you will need to enter your Apple ID or use your Face ID. Sometimes, the app you wish to download has previously been purchased by other family members if you are also a part of a Family Sharing group. While in the App Store, click on your name on the bottom-left-hand side of the page, and a list of all apps purchased using your Apple ID will be displayed. Next, to download the App, click on the "Purchased by" > family member's name> iCloud status icon beside the app.

Click on the app to see its details and then a sharing option to share an app.

Hide a Purchased App

To hide a purchased app, hold the pointer over an app, click the Show More button, and then choose Hide Purchase. To unhide a hidden app click on View Information> Manage> Unhide> Done.

Update Installed Apps

The moment an update is available for any of your downloaded Apps, a notification will be displayed in the Notifications Center. A badge will be visible on the App Store icon on the Home screen (with a number displayed indicating the number of updates available). From the updates pane in the Apps store, you have the option of updating all Apps (click Update All) or updating individual apps (click Update beside each app you intend to update). You can also update an app once you receive a notification that an updated version of the app is available or from the Apps store> Updates.

If you prefer that all your apps be automatically updated, App store> Preferences> Automatic Updates.

Re-Download an Uninstalled App

To reinstall a previously installed app that you uninstalled or deleted, navigate to Apps store> re-download the app by clicking the re-download button.

Uninstall an App

Move the app from the Applications folder to the Trash to uninstall an app. Once the Trash is emptied, the app is permanently removed. However, you can still get it back from the Trash before emptying by selecting Trash> File> Put Back. Also, from the Launchpad, hold an app till the other apps begin to move gently from side to side and click the visible Delete button (for apps purchased from App Store).

You can subscribe to Apple Arcade in the App store to access a vast collection of iPhone games. App store> Arcade> Start a free one-month subscription or Start a monthly subscription> Subscribe> Authorize with Apple Face Touch ID.

Note that the availability of an app in the App store is dependent on the country or region you are located in.

Lots of Games to Play With Your Friends on the iPhone

Go to App store> Games or Arcade or Enter the game's name in the search bar and download it as you would other apps. You can access your downloaded games and progress on other devices you are signed in to with the same Apple ID.

iTunes App

iTunes store allows you to access the world's largest music, films, and TV shows collection, listen to your collection of songs and organize the songs and albums you buy on iTunes in your library.

Once you buy or download music, it is updated in your music library, and any song that is not already in the Store is added to iCloud.

To add or download music to your device, launch the iTunes app and search the catalog (input a keyword that relates to the song in the search field). When you see the song of your choice in the search results, select the "More" button next to it and add it to the library or Download it. Downloading a song allows you to access it even when you are offline (not connected to the internet). You can also view recommendations of songs that were curated for you based on your listening history and preferences and "What's new" to find new songs.

Listen to Songs

To play songs, launch the music app, navigate to the song you wish to listen to, click on it and Play or Click on the song. You can use the controls to pause, repeat, play songs in a defined order or shuffle songs.

Share Music Library With Others

You can share with other users you authorize to (with a password).

iTunes allows you to buy, rent, and watch all your favorite movies and TV shows from any of your devices.

Search for Content

You can browse for content by clicking the Movies, TV shows, or Kids tab in the menu and then pick the genre and look through it. When you find the content you wish to watch, you have the option of buying or renting. You can also share with up to six family members through Family sharing.

Find My App

You must first link a missing iPhone to your Apple ID before using the Find My app to track it down.

Even if your iPhone is fully wiped, it has an Activation Lock function that prohibits anybody else from activating and using it. Activation Lock for iPhone, iPad, and iPod Touch is described on the Apple Support page.

Add Your iPhone

- Go to Settings> [your name]> Find My on your iPhone.

- Enter your Apple ID if prompted, or tap "Don't have an Apple ID or forget it?" if you don't have one.

- Then follow the on-screen prompts:

    ✓ Turn on Find My iPhone by tapping Find My iPhone.

    ✓ Select one of the following options:

        o **Find My network or Enable Offline Finding:** If your device is not connected to Wi-Fi or cellular, Find My can use Find My network to find it.

        o **Send Last Position:** Apple will automatically send its location to you if your device's battery charge level drops to a dangerously low level.

Add a Device Belonging to a Family Member

If you initially set up Family Sharing, you may view your family members' devices under Find My. In the Gadgets list, their devices show underneath yours. You can't add the devices of your pals to Find My. Friends who misplace a device may log in with their Apple ID at iCloud.com/find.

Music App

On the iPhone 13, the Music app is the created home for your music. While many applications provide music, the Music app is the only one they need for many individuals.

In the iOS Music App, look for a song or album: The Music app is a bit difficult to use at first, but once you get the hang of it, it's simple to explore your music collection until you locate the song, album, or playlist you like to hear to and touch it to play it.

- Open the Music app from the iPhone's Home screen.

- If the app does not launch on the Library screen, go to the bottom of the page and press Library.

- Choose one of the areas in the list—for example, Playlists, Artists, or Albums—to view the music choices in your music library that fall into that category.

- Tap Artists, for example, to get a list of music artists. To see music or albums you have on your iPhone or in iCloud, tap an artist's name. Select an album or single from the artist's discography.

- Similarly, select any of the sections on the Library screen.

- The Music app's main screen is the Library screen. Tap Library to revisit it at any moment.

How to Purchase Apple Music

Apple provides a premium streaming music service that adds 50 million songs to the Music app, as well as your complete music collection. Student, individual, and family plans are available after a free trial. When you sign up for Apple Music, you'll be able to listen to Subscriptions to Apple Music Apple provides a premium streaming music service that adds 50 million songs to the Music app, as well as your complete music collection. Student, individual, and family plans are available after a free trial.

A handful of new icons are located at the end of the Music App screen when you subscribe to Apple Music:

The "For You" screen displays music that Apple had chosen for you based on your choices when you signed up for Apple Music.

Browse features selected music in categories such as Top 100 lists, Hot Tracks, New Music, and more.

Although streaming music needs a Wi-Fi or cellular internet connection, you may download several songs as you want from Apple Music to your device and listen when you don't have access to one.

On iPhone 13, how can you purchase a song you like from Apple Music on the iTunes Store?

- On your iPhone, open the iTunes Store app.

- Search for anything particular in the store's featured or Charts sections, or explore the store's Featured or Charts sections.

- When you're viewing an album, touch on the amount to buy the whole album or a single song.

- Confirm your order.

If you have trouble remembering what songs you enjoy on Apple Music and want to buy later, make a playlist called "Songs to Buy" or something similar to ensure you understand what to search for.

How to Download Songs From Apple Music

You can download albums and songs from Apple Music and listen to them even if you don't have access to the internet.

- Launch the Apple Music application.

- Go online and look for the songs you want to download.

- Select any song, album, playlist, or music video and tap Add. It will be added to your library as a result of this. NB: The download symbol will now appear beside items in your library, which you may touch to start the download.

- Go to Settings and activate Automatic Downloads if you want to download music without adding it to your collection first. When you touch the + icon, you will be sent to a page where you may download anything right away.

The Library tab will store your downloads. Simply go to the center of the display and choose Download Music. It's broken down into playlists, artists, albums, and individual songs.

Chapter 6.
Camera

Camera Interface

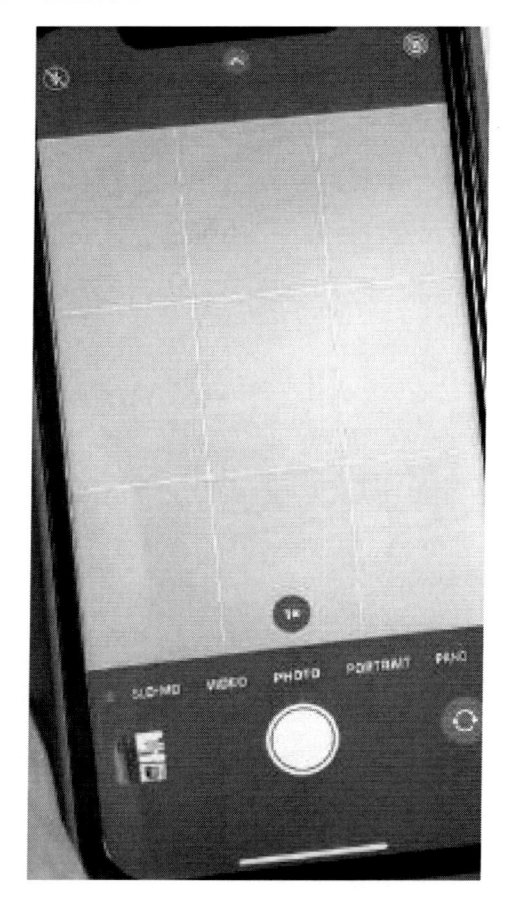

There are many things you can adjust before you take photos with the iPhone 13. These include:

- Video recording settings
- Photos
- Lighting settings
- Sound settings
- White balance

To find these settings, open up the camera app, hit the Camera button, and select Camera Settings. Then choose from among the various camera settings:

In this section, you can adjust how you want to capture photos, including the brightness, shutter speed, contrast, white balance, ISO, and exposure compensation. Some settings will allow you to change your camera mode.

When you're done, tap the Menu button in the top right corner of the iPhone 13's screen and tap Settings to go back to the iPhone 13's camera settings.

Camera Settings

iPhone cameras have several settings that can help you take a better-quality photo. You'll find these settings along the bottom of your camera screen.

ISO

This is the sensitivity setting of your camera. It's an indication of how sensitive the sensor is to light. The lower the number, the less sensitive it is. The lower the number, the greater the chance that the photo will have noise, artifacts, or other problems. The best range to be in is 100 to 800, although it's recommended that you not shoot below 100.

Shutter Speed

This is the amount of time that you give your camera to take a picture before it takes the photo. To make a photo, you will choose the camera and then either press the shutter button halfway down or press and hold the button down for the length of time you want to wait before taking the photo. For example, if you want a 30-second exposure, hold the button down for 30 seconds. Shutter speed is displayed in either a digital stopwatch or in a count of frames, or if you choose, a range between 0 and 30 seconds. When you're looking for the best shutter speed for your photo, experiment by adjusting it. When you make a photo, the fastest shutter speed possible is the best option.

Focus

This is what the camera does when it finds a subject to focus on. In general, the focus is set at one of two points, manual or autofocus. With a single focus point, your camera selects a focus point and places the image there. For a more precise focus, you can select manual focus, which allows you to manually focus a picture. When you point the camera at a specific subject and press the shutter button, it will choose the subject that is closest and best focused.

Autofocus

This works automatically, with the camera focusing on subjects in the frame. If you're not too good at using autofocus, it will often focus on the face of a person in a photo. With many other subjects, this can be a problem. Autofocus is an extra step you need to master, but it can lead to better pictures.

How to Use the Camera to Take Still Photos

- Open the camera app
- Focus the lens of the theory on the object you want to capture
- Then press the shutter button, and your photo will be saved immediately.

How to Use Live Focus

Live focus photography is a photography technique that produces photos with sharp, and crisp results. The camera app is able to adjust the background blur setting in real-time so that the background of the image is always clear.

There are four different live focus features in the camera app including:

1. **Auto Focus (AF):** This feature uses autofocus technology to adjust the camera's focus in real-time.
2. **Slow Focus (S):** When using this feature, the camera first takes a fast image, and then waits several seconds for the subject to enter the frame.
3. **Manual Focus (M):** It lets the user adjust the focus using the camera's ring.

    It lets the user adjust the focus using the camera's ring.
4. **Focus Stacking (C):** This feature lets the user take consecutive photos while focusing on different parts of a single subject.

Step 1: Select the Live Focus Mode

1. Open the Camera app.
2. Tap on the Live Focus icon.

Step 2: Pick the Live Focus Mode You Want to Use

1. Position the object and press the Shutter button.

How to Use Portrait Mode

1. Open your camera.

2. Search for Portrait Mode just above the Shutter button.

3. Then focus your camera on what you want to capture.

How to Take Pano Pictures

1. The first thing you do is unlock your phone, and open up Photos. You can do that by tapping on the icon in the bottom-left.

2. In Photos, you should see "Pano" in the upper right-hand corner. That's my default, and if you don't have that, then you can press the little circle to the right of Pano, or tap on the word Pano in the upper right-hand corner.

3. And that's about it. Then press "Take panorama," which is in the bottom-left of the screen.

4. You'll see the usual instructions: Press the shutter when the camera app says to, you'll have the option of zooming and shooting, and you'll have all the other settings.

5. You can then save the picture.

How to Take a Screenshot

To take a screenshot, just press the Sleep/Wake button and the Home button at the same time. This will save the screenshot into the iPhoto library.

You can also capture a screenshot of your iPhone or iPad screen using the same button combination or even just double-tap the Home button to make the screen snap.

You can also take screenshots of a live video by pressing the Power button and the Volume down button at the same time.

Take a Screenshot With Gestures

Your device allows you to take a screenshot with a gesture. With a double press of the Sleep/Wake button or by using the side button + Shift button, your iPhone will instantly capture all visible elements of the screen. If you want to take a screen capture of just a section of your screen, press and hold your finger in that area and your iPhone will automatically take a screenshot of that part of the screen.

Using Screen Recorder

The screen recorder is extremely easy to use. There is a dedicated icon on the screen that can record all your screen activities. You don't need to download and install any software. Just tap the icon and the screen is recorded in 4K quality (which you need to be connected to the Internet). After recording, you can replay the video, share it on the social networking site, and upload it for sharing and making presentations.

How to Record Screen on iPhone 13 Series

Just go to the Settings app and tap on Screen Time. Tap on Screen Time and tap on the Record button. Here, you will see the option to start or stop the recording. You can also delete the recording if required.

Also, you can do the same by going to the Control Center and tapping on the Rec button. The screen will record in 4K. You will be able to record for up to 30 minutes.

How to Take Videos

1. Open the Camera App.
2. Just above the Shutter button, you will see "Video" click on it.
3. Pressing the round circle icon (Shutter button) it will begin to display a little dot in between.
4. Then your video has started recording.
5. When you are done press the icon with the red dot in between to save the video.
6. The video will be immediately saved.

How to Scan QR Code With Your Camera

QR (QR bar code) or Quick Response bar code is a data matrix code and is also a type of 2D barcode. It is a popular and universal encoding standard used to create the links between products. The symbol of QR is actually a square QR code.

A QR code can be used on a phone, tablet, or any other device, which has a camera to recognize QR codes.

Some apps support QR codes including the camera app of your iPhone. You can take pictures with your camera app and scan a QR code. To use the QR code scanner in the camera app, follow the steps below:

1. **Step 1:** Open the camera app on iPhone 13 Pro Max. On iPhone XR, there will be no way to open the camera. You can only view images and videos on iPhone XS, XS Max, and XR.
2. **Step 2:** From the top row of the camera app, tap the Scanner icon. You will see that the bottom row has five

options:

- Use Photo Library
- Use All Schemes
- Custom Scan
- QR Code Scanner
- All Photos.

3. **Step 3:** Open the Camera app to select the QR code mode.

    Use the Photo Library to open the QR code mode.

4. **Step 4:** From the menu bar on the left side of the camera, tap the QR Code option, then tap either QR Code.

    If the QR Code is already scanned by the camera, it will appear on the screen. You can then edit the QR code. If you tap the QR Code option again, it will display the QR code reader, which is a bar code scanner. The QR code reader can be used for scanning all kinds of documents, text, QR codes, and bar codes.

    The QR code scanner will likely be the next best thing to the fingerprint scanner.

5. **Step 5:** From the QR code reader app, you can edit the bar code, such as edit QR code or remove it, and create new QR codes.

How to Use Picture-in-Picture

Picture-in-picture on iPhone 13 has its place in the user interface. It allows you to watch two different videos at the same time. You could watch a movie, play a video game or do anything else you want while being able to watch TV.

Using picture-in-picture on iPhone 13 allows you to:

- Watch movies while being able to talk on the phone.
- Watch movies while being able to listen to the radio.
- Watch movies while doing other stuff on your iPhone.
- Watch videos while doing other stuff on your iPhone.

To use picture-in-picture on iPhone 13, all you need to do is to tap on the Settings icon on the side of the display. Next, tap on the Picture-in-Picture option.

With picture-in-picture turned on, you'll see that it's now the first option in the settings menu for picture-in-picture. If you turn off picture-in-picture, you'll have to turn it on again.

Tap on picture-in-picture, and then tap on the blue arrow to enable picture-in-picture.

Once you're done, picture-in-picture will be enabled on your iPhone. You'll now see that the screen will be split into two parts. To start using picture-in-picture, you'll need to drag the image or video you want to watch up to the top-left portion of the screen. Once you've dragged the video there, you'll be able to see the video with the speaker icon in the top-left corner of the screen.

Next, you'll want to add an audio source from the music app. The audio can come from the phone's speaker or another connected speaker. To add an audio source, tap on the speaker icon.

The speaker icon will then become blue and you'll see the speaker icon appear in the top-left corner of the screen. Now, just tap on it to start the audio.

Also, you'll be able to control the volume of the audio, so you don't want to miss any important parts of the video or audio. In the next section, we'll explain how to control the volume.

How to Control Volume

If you're watching a video on the iPhone and you want to control the volume, you'll need to tap on the video. Next, you'll tap on the volume slider.

The slider will display the current volume level on the screen. You can control the volume by using the slider to turn it up or down.

That's it! That's how to make picture-in-picture on iPhone.

Chapter 7.

Music, Video, and the Latest News

News

Although a very high percentage of the world's population has a cell phone in their possession, the reality is that those who make the best use of these mobile technologies are the younger generations or, alternatively, professionals who, due to day-to-day dynamics, must be attentive to their teams during a good part of the day. Whatever the case, the widespread use of cell phones is not new. For just over 15 years, phones with these characteristics have been sold in bulk in all cities of the world. They are comfortable to wear, they keep us connected to things or events that interest us, as well as to people and loved ones whom we do not want to lose sight of.

The fact that mobile equipment technology has exploded in such a way should not surprise us, since it is the next logical step after the creation of local telephones and the exponential growth and expansion of the Internet. Now, among the many things in which Apple stands out is that its tools always have the user's security and privacy as a fundamental premise. Aside from this vision of the game, they have not neglected other sections such as entertainment (music, video, photography) and the possibility for its users to acquire all kinds of applications within the company's App Store.

The iPhone 13, which bears witness to past generations, is not exempt from this reality. Its technical characteristics represent a blow of authority on the table, allowing its users to be more comfortable with the functionalities while being able to stay connected at all times with any situation that is especially interesting or necessary for them.

First of all, a necessary mention of the growth of the entertainment industry in recent years. The same thing that has led the company to build solid alliances to guarantee the user a high-quality standard that, in turn, goes hand in hand with their needs as people.

Apple, iPhone, and Entertainment

Although it is true that a mobile device is an essential tool these days because of the opportunities it offers us to be in contact with people who in some way interest us, it is also true that enjoying a mobile device involves other alternatives that we cannot and should not omit under any circumstances. Apple has been characterized by its security, privacy, and its cameras. This is a rather reductive conclusion, often coming from people who have always bought equipment from other companies. The genuine Apple user recognizes that the iPhone, in its different generations, has been incorporating more and more new tools linked to entertainment and enjoyment.

Hence the importance of making a point when highlighting why the new iPhone 13 is above any equipment launched on the market by other companies. Its initial guarantees (security and privacy) are maintained, while new technical elements are incorporated for better equipment performance. Additionally, the applications available in the App Store are a clear indicator of the democratic nature with which Apple manages the entertainment possibilities of its users.

Some Applications Within the Apple Ecosystem for Video, Music, and News

Obviously, when we buy a device, it contains an operating system that gives it life. Some companies include the pre-installed applications, social networks, or prioritized platforms within the business idea of each corporation. With Apple, the dynamic is somewhat different. Although Apple does sell its products with some pre-installed tools, it also offers us the possibility of incorporating applications and other tools that we extract from the App Store. If companies like Google or Android do the same thing, what sets Apple apart from the rest? In essence, the rigorous quality control it carries out to prevent corrupted applications (malware) from being marketed within its App Store.

The latter means that, if you have purchased your iPhone 13 and want to incorporate some applications that you found in the App Store, you can do so in complete safety, since the company has previously made a considerable effort, to monitor the quality of all software products that are for sale or present within the Store. In this way, the possibility of you installing a malicious app that poses a threat to your personal data is reduced to a minimum. Next, we recommend some very interesting applications, all dedicated to managing music, video, and news.

App Music

Considered by many to be the most interesting and effective streaming music service in the world, Apple Music stands out due to its infinity of advantages compared to options such as Spotify or Tidal. The best way to define Apple Music is by comparing it with its most relevant competitors in the sector. These are some of the most significant advantages of the use of Apple Music within your iPhone 13.

- **Integration of your library:** Best of all, Apple Music is installed by default on all your devices in the Apple ecosystem. You do not need to download or install anything because, as it is an original product of the company, all the guarantees and conditions for its use are given. This facility is invaluable to all types of users, especially those who have used iTunes for years to manage their music library. If, in addition, you are someone very methodical and orderly, Apple Music allows you to incorporate all the songs you select into specific folders, attaching them to labels that you can edit to your taste.

- **It helps you discover interesting things:** Another feature that we have to highlight is that the platform uses an innovative bubble system to understand your musical tastes. Even if your experience within the platform begins without a fixed course, the artificial intelligence of Apple Music will readjust the songs that it offers to you based on the musical genre that you listen to most frequently.

- **Works as a social network:** We recognize that this sounds quite complicated, but it is not. Apple's primary idea is to give its platform superior branding. Far from becoming the best streaming music platform, they want to go much further, gradually turning it into a specific social network for artists.

This will allow you to feel closer to the musicians you have admired for years.

Splice

Splice is a free video editor that works on any device within Apple. If you are the type of user who loves to edit photos and videos, this alternative will leave you more than surprised. With it, you can join HD photos and videos to create a kind of movie that you can use at any time in your life. In fact, you can play it on your iPhone 13 or share it online if that's what you want. In any case, it provides a pleasant experience since it has an intuitive and friendly graphical interface. You don't need to be a very skilled graphic designer to work on your own creations.

Among its most important features stand out:

- Automatically synchronize your video with the rhythm of the music.
- Apply titles, layers, filters, and transitions.
- It has slow and fast motion effects.
- You can select music from iTunes.
- You can add voiceover effects to narrate your videos.
- Share on YouTube, Facebook, and Vimeo.

iMovie

It is impossible to make a list of the best video editors in the world without explaining, even superficially, the immense potential of this original Apple application. iMovie, a video editor that works for iPhones and iPad, allows you to create beautiful movies in HD format that you can play both on your trusted Apple devices and any other device with an iOS system. It is free, which provides a very important plus for many users. Although the application cannot be considered a tool for professionals in the area, it does reveal itself as a relevant alternative for beginner users who want to create, play and make trailers with a fairly acceptable quality standard.

Among its most special characteristics, the following stand out:

- More than 14 trailers for you to create your Hollywood movie to your liking.
- You can customize the logo of your movies, titles, and credits.
- 8 themes for titles, transitions, and music.
- 10 filters designed by Apple.
- Slow and fast motion, picture-in-picture, and split-screen effects.
- Share on YouTube, Facebook, and Vimeo.

As you may have noticed, applications are a key element for the entertainment of any mobile device. We selected these 3 for their security and because there is no possibility that their use will bring threats to the security of your device. Privacy, as a focal point in all the development and commercial strategies of the Apple Company, is claimed here at its best.

The foregoing arises, therefore, as a compelling reason for you to allow yourself the experience of browsing these applications with absolute confidence that you will not receive attacks or that the security of your device will be violated under any circumstance. You will be able to edit videos, take the best photographs and be aware of what is happening in the world without any risk to your privacy. This is what makes Apple a company that will forever be recorded in the annals of history, not only of business history but of innovation and the development of new ways of relating to each other.

Chapter 8.
Web and Communication

Safari

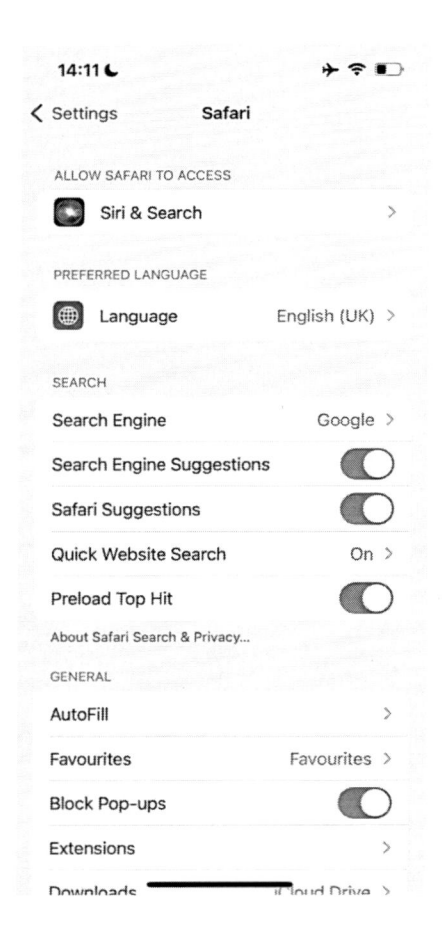

Safari has a new look in iOS 15. Controls are relocated to the bottom of the screen, making them simpler to grasp with one hand.

A new, compact tab bar floats at the bottom of the screen, allowing users to slide between tabs effortlessly, and it also includes a Smart Search box. Tab Groups allow users to keep their tabs in a folder and sync them across iPhone, iPad, and Mac devices. The presence of a new tab overview grid view.

Weather

In iOS 15, the Weather app has been completely revamped. The Weather app now has more graphical weather data displays, a full-screen map, and a dynamic layout depending on outside circumstances.

Apple has updated the animated backdrops in the Weather app to better properly represent the sun's current position and precipitation conditions. Also, there are additional alerts that indicate when rain or snow begins and ends.

How to Disable Safari's Website Tinting

Tinting occurs when the Safari color interface changes to match the color format of the website you're viewing in the tabs, bookmarks, and navigation button sections.

Tinting allows the browser interface to fade into the background, creating a more immersive experience. However, the effect is not universally liked, and some people are turned off by it. Fortunately, Apple included a toggle switch to disable it.

1. On your iPhone, open the Settings app.
2. Scroll to the lower part and hit Safari.
3. Turn off the option next to Allow Website Tinting in the "Tabs" section.

4. Move Safari's Address Search Field to Top Section.

5. On the address bar's left side, press the "aA" symbol.

6. In the popup menu, choose Show Top Address Bar.

Additionally, you can manage this design change under Safari's "Tabs" section of Settings>Safari. Select Single Tab to move the URL bar to the top.

1. Download and Install Web Extensions for Safari

2. Open Settings.

3. Scroll to the lower part and hit Safari.

4. Select Extensions from the "General" menu.

5. Select more Extensions.

This last step will lead you to an App Store area devoted to Safari extensions, where you can explore and, if desired, download and install them. Please keep in mind that although some extensions are free, some contain features that need in-app payments to activate.

Once an extension is installed, it will appear in the Settings' "Extensions" section, where you can manage any extension-related settings.

Quickly Refresh Safari Web Page

Apple has retained the refresh symbol in the address bar, which you can touch to reload the currently viewed website. However, there is now another, less apparent method of refreshing websites that you can find more conveniently. In Safari, all it takes to refresh a website is a downward swipe on any page. This alternative to pressing on the reload symbol is particularly helpful if you want to preserve the address bar by the top of the screen, where tapping on the reload icon is inconvenient.

How to Customize the Start Page and Background of Safari

The Start Page has many configurable elements, such as the ability to customize the Start Page background. Additionally, you can sync the look of your Start Page across all of your devices through iCloud. The following instructions demonstrate how to customize the Safari Start Page.

1. Open Safari on your iPhone or iPad.

2. In the down-right corner of the Safari screen, press the Open Tabs symbol.

3. To start a new tab in the Tabs view, touch the Plus symbol in the lower-left corner.

4. At the bottom of the Start Page, scroll down and touch the Edit button.

5. Turn on the option next to Use Start Page on All Devices to sync your Start Page settings with additional devices associated with the same Apple ID.

6. Utilize the controls to customize what appears on your Start Page. Favorites, Reading List, Privacy Report, Siri Suggestions, Frequently Visited, Shared with You, and iCloud Tabs are all available choices. Also, you can enable the Background picture option and choose one of the pre-installed iOS wallpapers or create your own by pressing the large Plus icon.

7. When finished, press the X in the top-right corner of the menu card.

Delete Tabs Group

When a Tab Group is no longer required, it is simple to remove it.

1. Press the Open Tabs button in the lower right corner of the screen when reading a website.
2. At the lower part of the screen, touch the tab bar in the center.
3. In the upper left corner of the menu card, touch Edit.
4. To delete a Tab Group, touch the circular ellipsis symbol next to it, then touch Delete.

How to Make Your IP Address Untraceable

1. Open the Settings app.
2. Scroll to the bottom and hit Safari.
3. Scroll down and hit Hide IP address under the "Privacy and Security" section.
4. Choose between Trackers and Websites or just Trackers.

FaceTime

Set Up iPhone FaceTime

Go to FaceTime Settings, then toggle FaceTime on.

Do any of these:

- Set up your FaceTime calling account: Click use your FaceTime Apple ID, then click Sign In.Note: You can create one if you do not have an Apple ID.
- In calls, to highlight the speaker: Turn the speech on.
- In FaceTime chats, to take live photos: Turn FaceTime Live Photos on.

- Activate FaceTime Call
- Ask Siri. "Make a FaceTime call."
- Tap New FaceTime at the top of the screen in FaceTime.
- In the input area above, type the name or number that you wish to call. Then, click the FaceTime icon to make a video call or the Audio call button (not available in all countries or regions).
- You may also hit the Contact Add button to open contacts and add persons or tap a suggested call history contact to make a quick call.

Tip: Rotate iPhone to use landscape orientation to view more during a FaceTime video chat.

Receive a FaceTime Call

Tap any of the following when a FaceTime call comes in:

- Take the call: Drag the tap Accept or drag the slider.
- Remove call: Press Decline.
- Set a callback reminder: Press remind Me.
- Send your caller an SMS message: Tap Message.

The screen for the incoming call. The Remember Me and Message buttons are at the bottom of the screen, in the top row, from left to right. The Decline and Accept buttons are on the bottom row from left to right.

Rather than accept, you see the End and Accept option, which ends the previous call and links you to the incoming call when another call comes in.

Tip: You can have Siri advised to accept or refuse incoming calls by your voice.

Start a Facetime Conversation Call From Messages

You can initiate a facetime call in a message conversation with the person with whom you are chatting.

At the top right corner of the Message chat press the FaceTime button.

Do any of these:

- Tap Audio FaceTime.
- Tap Video FaceTime.

Submit a Message

Do one of the following if no one answers your FaceTime call:

- Click leave Message.
- Click Cancel.
- Tap call back.

Call Again

Tap the name or number of the individual(s) you wish to call again in your call history.

FaceTime Sound Settings

The FaceTime app's spatial audio sounds like you have friends in your room. However, their voices are dispersed and sound like they come from every individual's direction on the screen.

Note: Space audio is available on supported models only.

Filter Sounds From the Background

You can turn on Voice Isolation mode if you want your voice heard clearly in FaceTime and extraneous sounds filtered out (available on supported models). Voice isolation priority in FaceTime betters your voice and blocks environmental noise.

- Open Control Center, press Mic Mode, and select Voice Isolation during a FaceTime chat.

Enable All Sounds During Facetime

You can turn on Wide Spectrum Mode if you want your voice and all sounds in a FaceTime call (available on supported models).

- Open the Control Center, touch Mic Mode and choose Wide Spectrum during a FaceTime call.

Switch the Sound Off

- Hit the screen for FaceTime (if not shown), and then tap the Mute Off button to turn off the sound. Next, make a selection of the FaceTime controls.

- Tap the button again to reactivate the sound.

If your sound is turned off, your mic will detect if you talk and notify you that your microphone is silent and that you can hit the On button to enable it.

View FaceTime Participants in a Grid Structure

You can observe participants in tiles of the same size grouped in a grid during a chat with 4 or more persons in the FaceTime app. Tile of the speaker is immediately highlighted, so who speaks is easy to know. (Some tiles may seem fuzzy depending on your model.)

- Tap the Grid button in the lower-left corner of the screen in a FaceTime call (if you can't see the button, tap the screen).

- Tap it again to turn the grid off.

Create a Link to a FaceTime Call

With the iPhone FaceTime app, you can link a FaceTime call and send a link (through mail or messages) to a friend or group, which can be used to join or initiate a call.

- Tap Creating Link close to the screen top.
- Select an option to send the URL (Mail, Messages, and so on).

Chapter 9.

Utilities and Maps App

Using Maps

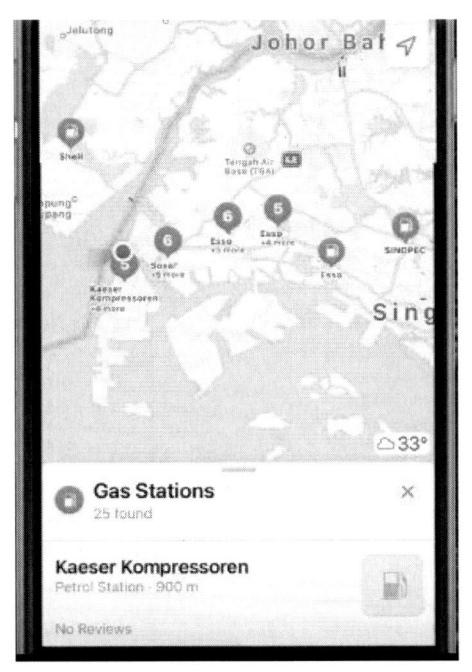

Apple maps and the navigation system in Apple iPhone are developed based on Apple's own mapping technology, called C3, which was first introduced in Google Maps for Android. Apple maps are developed with extensive use of the existing Map Kit framework which is a framework developed by Apple for iPhone navigation system development. Apple maps use GPS, Wi-Fi, accelerometer data, and other sensors in the iPhone for providing accurate and real-time navigation.

Using the Apple Maps on iPhone, the users can access various information about the real estate, hospitals, shopping malls, petrol pumps, coffee shops, restaurants, banks, ATMs, and more from the map. By using Apple Map, iPhone users can explore and drive around the whole city effectively and reliably.

What Is Apple Maps App?

Apple Maps is the official map app developed by Apple which is integrated with the iPhone and it's integrated with the iOS operating system. There are 2 types of maps that are Apple Maps and Google Maps, the Apple Maps are used only by the iPhone users while Google Maps are integrated with the Android OS operating system and other mobile phone devices.

Apple Maps is a native map app for iPhone which means it uses iPhone hardware features for providing maps and driving directions. Apple Maps use the GPS and other GPS sensors in the iPhone for providing accurate maps and driving directions. Apple Maps also use the accelerometer and gyroscope sensors, which provide accurate and real-time maps for driving directions.

Apple Maps also use Wi-Fi connectivity and the Apple maps app also uses the Apple maps data to determine the locations of restaurants, shopping centers, and petrol pumps for iPhone users. These locations are not available in the iPhone search bar while the app is being downloaded on the iPhone.

It's also important to note that by using Apple Maps on iPhone, iPhone users can access their location. Using this, iPhone users can access the driving directions and the list of their favorite places, and it's also one of the fastest navigation apps in the iOS marketplace. The Apple Maps app was launched with iPhone 4S and it's available for all iOS devices.

Google Maps

Google Maps on iPhone is the app to know for any iPhone user. The app has been very successful and has more than 4 million downloads. It is an app that has become very popular.

The app makes use of your location and shows you the maps with directions on how to get to any place, including directions on how to get to that place from any other place. The app has also been updated very frequently. All this together makes the app more attractive and useful.

Downloading the Google Maps for iPhone App

The app is currently available to all iPhone users with a 3G connection. It is also available to users who have a 4G connection. You download the app from the Apple App Store.

The first maps app is not exactly an alternative to the Apple maps app, but it is an app that many people are using when they are driving or want to go to places around.

Google Maps can be used on the iPhone using the Apple Maps app. To do this, users have to click and drag the location they want on the map and get the maps displayed on the iPhone with the selected location on it.

You will then click on the direction menu on the iPhone to get a map of the direction. You can then click on the destination to go there.

Apple has not released Google Maps on the iPhone but there are ways you can get the same.

You can search for locations on Google Maps on your iPhone on the web. You will need to have an internet connection and you will need to search for a location that is not too far from where you are.

You can use the map with the selected location you found. You can then click on the direction menu to get a map of the directions. You can then click on the destination to go there.

How to Share Your Location

1. **Step 1: Open Google Maps.** Open the Google Maps app on your iPhone.

2. **Step 2: Tap the Compass button on the top right corner.** Open the compass icon from the top right corner of Google Maps.

3. **Step 3:Tap the Share Location button.** You can easily find the share location button on the map. Open the share location button and tap it.

4. **Step 4:Select the map.** After selecting the map, you can select either your current location or select one of your previous locations.

5. **Step 5: Tap the Share Location button.** When you select one of your previous locations, Google will ask you whether you want to add your location to your previous location.

6. **Step 6:Select your location or your previous location.** If you select your current location, Google Maps will start searching for the location on Google Maps. It will display a list of nearby places and ask you to confirm it.

7. **Step 7:Tap the desired location on the map.** When you confirm the location, Google Maps will display the location on the map.

8. **Step 8:Tap to share.** If you want to share your location with friends and family on Google Maps, you can tap the "Share your location" button. The location of your location will be displayed on Google Maps on the map along with other locations.

Calculating the Location of an Address

To get the directions, you just need to specify the starting address and ending address.

Also, using the "Route" option, you will be able to see a route map (in your case, probably as a list of address points) and you can get driving, walking, and public transport directions.

How to Set up Voice Mail

1. **Step 1:Open the Settings app.** Tap the Settings app, and then go to Phone>Voicemail>Voicemail settings.

2. **Step 2: If you have no voicemail account.** If you have no voicemail account, tap the Create new voicemail account and then set the voicemail password for your account.

   If you have one voicemail account already, you can also change the voicemail account on the same screen.

3. **Step 3: Set up the voicemail settings.** On the voicemail settings, you can set up the voicemail greeting, voicemail forward/back, and voicemail alert/vibration. You can choose whether you want to receive voicemail when a new voicemail comes, or only when your phone rings.

4. **Step 4: Create and use a new voicemail account.** If you have no voicemail account, tap the Create new voicemail account button, and set up a new voicemail account.

If you already have an account, tap the Use existing voicemail account button, and then enter the account number.

5. **Step 5: Test.** You can now use the voicemail message that was set in the last step.

   If the voicemail isn't working correctly, you can tap More> Call recording and tap Set as new voicemail.

   This will make it your new voicemail account.

On iPhone, you can also receive voicemail through the speaker and see voicemail on the Lock screen. To set this up, tap the icon in the upper right corner of your Lock screen and select the voicemail option.

Tapping it will display a list of the voicemail accounts you have, and you can add a new voicemail account here. You can see the voicemail transcript on the Lock screen and the ability to use your voice to respond to a voicemail.

Chapter 10.

Health and Fitness

Health

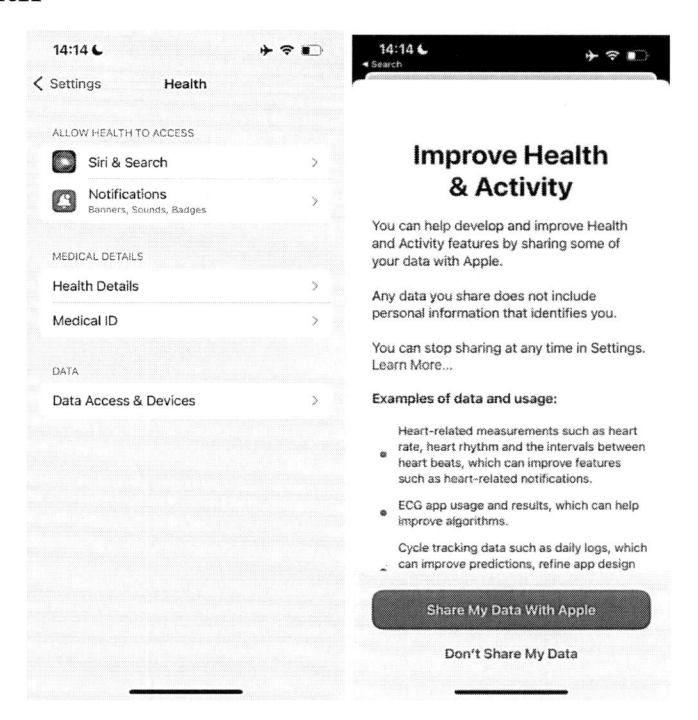

The Health app in iOS 15 now has a new sharing option that allows users to share their selected health data with family or carers. Descriptions, highlights, and the ability to pin findings for fast-access have been added to lab results. In addition, health can now detect

Trends, alerting users to significant changes in personal health indicators.

Walking Steadiness is a new statistic added to the Health app to reduce fall risk. COVID using a QR code from a healthcare practitioner, 19 vaccinations and test results may be saved in the Health app. Blood glucose features entail interactive charts and illustrate values across sleep and activity.

Add Health Data to iPhone Manually

Data such as measurements, symptoms, and menstrual cycle data can be entered manually in the Health App.

To view the screen for Health Categories, tap Browse at the bottom right and proceed as follows:

- Click a category (Scroll down to all categories.)
- Click the search field and enter the name of a category or a specific data type (such as body measurements) (such as weight).

Do any of these:

Include info to the Cycle Tracking category.

- In the Sleep category, add information: Tap Add Data in the upper right-hand corner.
- To other categories, add info: To edit the data, hit the Details icon and tap Add Data on the upper right.

Monitor Walking Steadiness

The health application employs special algorithms to analyze balance, strength, and gait when carrying your iPhone in the pocket or holder close to your waist. If your steadiness becomes poor or remains low, you might receive a notification and share it immediately with someone near you. Health can also show you practice to increase the stability of your walking.

Get Notifications for Low or Very Poor Steadiness

1. Tap the photo in the top right corner of your profile or initials.

2. Tap Summary or Browse at the bottom of the screen, and then scroll to the top of the screen if you don't see your profile or initials.

3. Click Health Checklist.

4. Tap Setup for walking stability notifications and then follow the directions in the display.

5. Tap Mobility, scroll down, and then tap Walking Steadiness Notices, to review your notifications.

See Your Data for Walking Steadiness

1. Tap Browse in the lower right and then tap Mobility.

2. Click Walking Steadiness (you may need to scroll down).

3. Click the Show Information button to learn about the 3 levels of steadiness (Low, Very Low, and OK).

See Health Trends

Once data have been collected over sufficient time, the health system can notify you of important changes in data categories such as heart rate rest, the number of steps, and amount of sleep. Trend lines indicate how much and how long certain metrics have changed.

To see all the latest trends, tap Summary at the bottom of the left.

You can do the following if health has identified trends:

- See more trend data: Tap graph.

- See further trends: Click see Health trends.

- Summary screen trend data comprising sleep graphs, Blood Glucose graphs, and rest heart rate.

- Hit Health Trends in the Summary Screen, tap "Manage notifications" to receive notifications about your health patterns, and then set Trends on.

View Highlights

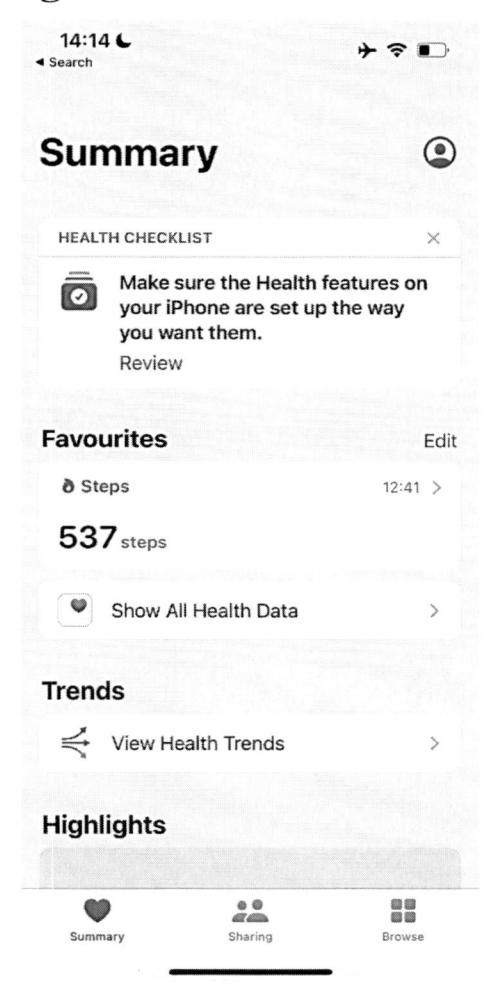

- To see highlights of your health and fitness, click Summary at the bottom left.

- Tap the Details button to view additional details about a highlight.

A summary screen presenting highlights including minutes of exercise and sleeping blood glucose.

Create Memoji

You can choose a custom Memoji, skin tone, hat, spectacles, and more. In addition, for different moods, you can create several Memoji.

The Memoji screen displays the character formed at the top and is customized below the selected feature options below. The button Done is on the right top, and the button Cancel is on the left top.

1. Tap the Memoji stickers button and click on the New Memoji button during the chat.

2. Tap every feature and select your preferences. By adding characteristics to your Memoji, your character comes alive.

3. To add Memoji to your collection, tap Done.

4. To modify, duplicate or delete a Memoji, click the Memoji Stickers button, press Memoji, and tap the More Options button.

Send Memoji Stickers

Sticker packs depending on your Memoji and Memoji characters are automatically generated. You may use stickers in unique ways to communicate several emotions.

1. Tap the Memoji Stickers button during a conversation.

2. To view the stickers in the sticker pack, tap the Memoji on the top row.

To send a sticker do this:

1. To add a sticker to the message bubble, tap the sticker. Then, tap the Send button to send if you like, and add a comment.

2. Touch a sticker and hold it and drag it to the top of the statement. When you add it to the message, the sticker will be sent instantly.

Memoji Recordings and Animated Memoji

You can send Memoji messages using your voice and reflect your facial emotions on compatible models.

1. Tap the Memoji button and select a Memoji in a chat.
2. To register your face and voice, use the Record button. To stop recording, tap the red square.
3. To check your message, tap Replay.
4. To send a message, tap the Send button, or delete to cancel.

Configure iPhone Focus

Concentration is a function that allows you to focus on a task by reducing distractions. Focus can temporarily stop any notifications or just enable certain notifications (for instance, those corresponding to your task)— and let other people and applications know that you are occupied.

You can select or build your Focus from the giving list.

Note: Open the control center, press Focus, then toggle on Do not disturb to silence all notifications swiftly. Do not disturb or do not disturb when driving is included in focusing now.

Set Focus

You can set a given focus option, such as driving, personal, sleep or work, or build an individual focus if you wish to focus on any specific activity. You can silence notifications or just allow people and applications notifications to fit your Focus—set up a Work Focus, for example, and only let your colleagues and work apps be enabled.

You can also customize a home page with only related applications connected to your Focus, which will make this page the only one available during your Focus.

Five focus alternatives were shown on a screen—don't interfere, drive, work, personal, and sleep. You may utilize the same Focus Settings on all your Apple devices with the same Apple ID on the Share Across devices button.

1. Enter settings>Click Focus.

2. For example, tap Focus—such as do not disturb, drive, work, sleep, or personal—then follow the instructions onscreen.

3. You can always return to Settings> Focus and alter anything you want after setting your Focus (which is initially specified when creating your Focus.

4. Choose (if any) people during focus who you prefer to get notifications. Press People or Add Person, Select Contacts and click Done.

5. Choose if you wish to receive calls during this Focus: Tap Calls from then choose —Favorites Everyone, No One, and All Contacts. Allow repeated calls to be activated (two or more calls within 3 minutes by the same person).

6. Finally, tap the Return button in the top right-hand corner.

    Note: Calls from your emergency contacts can always be received regardless of your focus settings.

7. Select applications during Focus from which you want (if any) notifications: Tap Apps or Add Apps, choose Apps, and tap Done.

8. Select if you wish to allow all apps during this Focus to get time-sensitive notifications immediately: Switch on Time Sensitive and press Back at the upper left.

9. Choose if you want apps to show quiet notifications: Tap Focus Status, then activate or deactivate Share Focus Status. When you activate it, people will see that you have silence notifications, but not which Focus you have enabled.

10. Select (if applicable) the home screen pages you want to visit in Focus: Click Home Screen, switch on a custom page, select a home page you want to utilize, and hit Done.

    Tip: The applications for this Focus can be moved to one home screen page and then pick that page.

11. Enable silenced notices on the lock screen or dim lock screen: Click Lock Screen, then switch on Show on Lock Screen. Dim Lock Screen may also be activated in this Focus to dim the lock screen.

Check Weather Conditions

The weather screen shows the location on the top and the current climate and temperature.

To do the following, Open Weather:

1. Check the local weather conditions: When you open the weather you will get the details for your present location.

2. The top of the screen shows updates on severe circumstances such as winter storms and flash floods. Tap to read the entire government warning (not available in all countries or regions).

3. See hourly Forecast: Turn left or right on the hourly display.

4. See 10-day forecast: See the weather, precipitation, and high and low temperatures for upcoming days.

5. Details on air quality: See information on air quality; tap See More for information on health and contaminants (not available in all countries or regions).

Note: When air quality reaches a given level, the air quality scale appears above the hourly forecast. The air quality scale is always above the hourly forecast in some regions.

6. Look at your area's weather maps: View a map of the surrounding temperature, rainfall, or air quality. Tap on the map for a full-screen view or alter the map view for air quality, temperature, and precipitation.

7. Further details More weather: Check the UV index, wind speed, sunrise, sunset, and more when you scroll down.

8. In other places, check the weather: Wipe the screen to the left or right, or tap the icon for Edit Cities.

How to Read Full-Screen Air Quality, Precipitation, and Temperature Maps

Turn on the weather map or Show Map icon to accomplish any of the following:

1. Tap the Overlaying menu button to modify the map display to temperature, rainfall, or air quality.

2. To move the map, tap the screen and drag the finger.

3. If you want to zoom in and out, pinch the screen.

4. Zoom out to view the 12-hour precipitation provision while looking at the precipitation map; zoom back to see the next-hour precipitation prediction (not available in all nations or regions).

5. To see a different place in your weather list, tap the Favorite Locations icon.

6. To return to your present location, tap the Current Location icon.

7. Click and hold the place to add it to your weather list, see its current conditions or view it in Maps.

8. The surrounding area is filled with a temperature map. The current location and preferred location buttons are in the upper right corner from top to bottom. In the center of the screen, you will find the following buttons on the menu to modify the display: Temperature, Air Quality, and Precipitation. The Done icon is in the upper left corner.

9. To go back to weather and forecast, tap Done.

Organize Reminder Lists

Creating, Editing, or Deleting Lists and Groups

In lists and groupings, you can categorize your reminders such as business, school, or purchase. Do any of these:

- Creating fresh list: Click add list, select an account, input a name, then select a color and symbol for the list if you have more than one account.

- Create a group list: Tap Edit, touch Add Group, enter a name, and then tap Create. Or drag a list to a different list.

- Set up lists and groups: Touch, hold, and drag a list or group to a new place. You can even transfer a list to another group.

- Modify a list or group name and appearance: Go to the left list or group, then hit Edit Details.

- Delete a list or group including reminders: Move then tap the Delete button on the list or group.

Use Tags

Tags can organize your reminders quickly and flexibly. You can just search for or filter reminders throughout your lists with one or more tags such as #shopping and #work.

- **Add tag:** Type #, write a tag name or pick a tag from the menu above the keyboard when creating or editing a reminder. A tag can only be one word, but it can be combined with dashes and underscores. You can add several tags to your reminder.

- **See reminders using tags:** Type a tag or All Tags in the Tag Browser (under your custom list). Then, tap more tags at the top of the list to filter the list further.

A screen that displays several lists of reminders and smart lists. The browser tag is in the lower part.

Chapter 11.

Siri

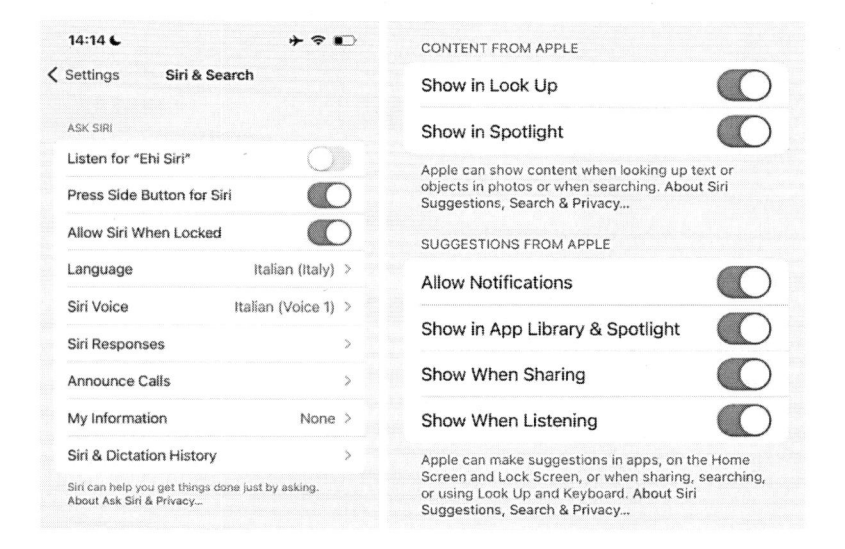

Siri queries in iOS 15 are handled on-device utilizing the Neural Engine, enhancing security and considerably increasing responsiveness while also eliminating the need for an internet connection.

As you use your smartphone, on-device speech recognition and understanding improve. Siri may also learn about the contacts you engage with the most, new phrases you write, and subjects you read about to deliver more relevant replies.

Siri can now transmit images, web pages, material from Apple Music or Apple Podcasts, Apple News stories, Maps locations, and other onscreen things in a Message, or even capture a screenshot to send. Furthermore, Siri may now utilize onscreen context to send a message or make a phone call.

Siri is now better at retaining context between requests, allowing you to refer to what you previously requested in a discussion. You may also make requests to operate a HomeKit gadget at a certain time or under specific conditions, like when you leave the house.

On AirPods and in Apple CarPlay, Siri may also Announce Notifications like Reminders, and users can ask Siri what is on their screen.

Siri can now deliver neural text-to-speech voice in more languages like Swedish, Danish, Norwegian, and Finnish. Siri also supports Mixed English, Indic, and a blend of Indian English and a native tongue, such as Hindi, Telugu, Kannada, Marathi, Tamil, Bengali, Gujarati, Malayalam, and Punjabi.

How to Instruct Siri to Control Your HomeKit Devices at a Predetermined Time

For example, if you want your blinds to open at 7 a.m. the next day, you might tell Siri, "Hey Siri, open the blinds at 7 a.m." Siri responds to geolocation instructions as well, so you can say things like, "Hey Siri, turn off the lights when I leave."

When you ask Siri to operate a HomeKit product in this manner, automation is created in the Home app's "Automation" section. If you wish to delete an Automation generated by Siri in the Home app, simply slide left and hit Delete.

In iOS 15, HomeKit developers may also add Siri functionality to their goods. However, it should be noted that using Siri commands with third-party devices necessitates the ownership of a HomePod to pass the requests through.

Third-party HomeKit gadgets that have Siri integration can be managed using Siri commands for tasks like scheduling reminders, controlling devices, broadcasting messages, and more.

How to Use Siri While Not Connected

You don't need to turn anything on for Siri to work offline once you've upgraded to iOS 15. The following are the sorts of queries that you can process without contacting Apple's servers:

- Timers and alarms can be set and deactivated.
- Start the applications.
- Control the audio playback of Apple Music and Podcasts.
- Control system settings like accessibility features, volume, Low Power Mode, and Airplane mode, among other things.

If you ask Siri to do something that requires internet access—such as messaging someone, getting weather updates, or watching a video—and you don't have a cellular data or Wi-Fi connection, you'll get a response like "To do that, you'll need to be online" or "I can help with that when you're connected to the internet."

How to Make Siri Read Your Notifications

In iOS 15, here's how you get Siri to announce alerts.

1. Open the Settings app.
2. Select Notifications.
3. Choose Announce Notifications via the "Siri" menu.

4. Toggle the switch next to Announce Notifications to the ON position in the green.

To have Siri broadcast all notifications from a single app, just choose it from the "Announce Notifications" from the list and enable the Announce Notifications option.

Chapter 12.

Setting Troubleshooting

Using a Computer Backup, Restore Your iPhone

1. Connect a fresh or recently wiped iPhone to the computer that has your backup via USB.

2. Choose one of the following options:

    a. On your Mac, in the Finder sidebar, type: After selecting your iPhone, click Trust.

    b. If you have several devices connected to your PC and are using the iTunes app on a Windows PC, click the device icon at the top left of the iTunes window, then pick your new or recently wiped iPhone from the list.

3. Click "Restore from this backup" on the welcome page, select your backup from the list, and then click Continue.

If your backup is password-protected, you'll need to input it before you can restore your data and settings.

How to Update iOS

Apple has launched iOS 15, the latest operating software update for iPhones. It brings many improvements to the quality of life while also fixing several issues from the previous version.

Let's look at how to get iOS 15 on your iPhone.

The following are the procedures you must follow to upgrade your iPhone to iOS 15:

1. Go to the Settings app and choose it.
2. Go to the "General" tab.
3. Choose "Software Update" from the drop-down menu.
4. At the bottom of the display, choose "Upgrade to iOS 15."
5. Select "Download and Install" from the drop-down menu.

You may read the entire comprehensive patch notes for iOS 15 while you're on the download page.

In addition to audio and video improvements for FaceTime, iOS 15 includes a notification overhaul and fixes several issues.

Ensure you understand all the changes and the Terms of Service before proceeding since there is no way to undo the update once it has been implemented. 3.24 GB of free space is required for the iOS 15 upgrade.

How to Restart Your Device

iPhones may be a nuisance at times. They become unresponsive or crash unexpectedly. Sometimes, you simply want to give your phone a new lease of life, and that's when restarting comes into play.

To switch off and restart your smartphone, all you have to do is press and hold either the volume button or the side power button until the power off slider displays. It's as simple as swiping it to turn the gadget off, then turning it back on.

How to Force Restart

Force restarting it if the screen is sluggish or has stopped, on the other hand, is a whole other story. Because you can't technically remove the battery from the phone, you'll have to depend on Apple's built-in software to assist you.

Press and rapidly remove the volume up button, and press and fast release the volume down button, after which tap and hold the side power button to restart your iPhone 13 forcibly. When the Apple logo displays, press and hold the button to force your phone to restart.

If difficulties continue, you'll need to call Apple support or take your device to an Apple shop, where a professional will be able to assist you.

Chapter 13.

Tips and Tricks

A Revamped Design

This iPhone 13 new function is presently the talk of the town. Predicated on the speculations, Apple will be revamping the complete appearance and feel of iPhone 13 (red) having a curved screen; this may produce it the first iPhone to truly have a curved screen. Furthermore, the non-public home button can also be removed from the body and will be changed by an ID.

Prioritize Your Downloads

Does it ever eventually assist you if you're installing multiple applications and wish to prioritize them? The newest iOS makes it happen rapidly. This feature will certainly let you take full advantage of the iPhone 13. While downloading multiple apps, long-press the 3D Touch Identification on your device; this will start another menu. Here, you can touch around the "Prioritize Downloads" substitute for customizing.

Rearrange How You Share Your Write-Ups

That is probably one of the most uncommon iPhone 13 tips that folks are sure you won't be familiar with. Once you share a sheet or any other sort of content material, you get assorted options within the screen. Ideally, users have to scroll to choose their preferred decision. You can customize this with a straight pull and drop. Whatever you surely got to do is long-press the choice and move it to rearrange your shortcuts.

Drag Sketches Within Your Message

The feature was introduced for Apple Watch, but soon became a fundamental element of the iOS 10 version. We also expect it to become there on iPhone 13 as well. To include sketches inside your message, start the app as if drafting an email faucet for the sketch icon (center with two fingertips); this will start a new interface you can use to pull sketches. You can either make a whole new sketch or drag something on a preexisting image, as well.

Change the Capturing Path in Panoramas

That is perhaps one of the most crucial iPhone 13 options for all of the camera lovers out there. For most of the period, we think that panoramas include a place shooting path (i.e., from left to right); this might surprise you; nevertheless, you can transform the shooting path with a person tap. Just start your camera and enter its panorama setting. Now, touch the arrow to change the shooting path.

Pressure Delicate Display

This iPhone 13 new function could make the brand-new device a substantial stunner. The OLED screen may very well be pressure-sensitive. Not only will it provide a brighter and broader take a look at an angle, but it'll get the touch more delicate. We noticed a pressure delicate screen in Galaxy S8, and Apple will probably redefine it in its young flagship phone as well.

Look for Words While Browsing

This trick will certainly let you keep your time and effort. After starting any website on Safari, it is possible to go to a term without starting another tab. Just pick the word that you want to search; this will start with an URL bar at the bottom of the record. Here, don't faucet on "Go." Just scroll down slightly to look at the option to get the phrase.

Bring Shortcuts for Emojis

Who doesn't like Emojis, right? In the long run, they'll be the new method of communication; this might surprise you; nevertheless, you can post Emojis using a shortcut as well. To accomplish this, visit your phone's Configurations and head to General> Keypad> Keyboards> Add New Keypad> Emoji. After adding the Emoji keypad, head to General> Keypad> Add New Shortcut, to put an Emoji rather than a term like a shortcut.

Save your settings and leave. Afterward, every time you will write the word, it'll automatically be considered the provided Emoji.

Require Arbitrary Passwords From Siri

We can't list away iPhone 13 tips without including several Siri tricks. If you wish to make a fresh and secure account password, but can't think about anything, you can take assistance from Siri. Just beginning Siri and state "Random Account password." Siri has a selection of alphanumeric passwords. Furthermore, you can restrict the number of character types in the account password (for instance, "Random account password 16 digits").

Adjust the Flashlight

This fancy feature lets you make a lot of the iPhone 13, once you are in the night. If needed, you can transform the effectiveness of your torch relating to your environment. To accomplish this, go directly to the Control Center and force touch over the torch option; this gives the next display you should use to change the effectiveness of the light. You can also push touch other symbols here to get added options.

Cellular and Photovoltaic Charger

That is only speculation, but if it is true, then Apple could have the capability to change the sport in the smartphone industry. Not only is usually iPhone 13 apt to be charged wirelessly; however, the rumor has it that it has a photovoltaic charging dish. It could be the 1st device of its kind that can charge its battery pack from an inbuilt photovoltaic dish. Now, the majority of us need to restrain for two months to understand how a large amount of this speculation will be true.

Correct Siri's Pronunciation

The same as humans, Siri can offer the wrong pronunciation of the term (mainly names). You can teach Siri the proper pronunciation by just saying, "That's not how you pronounce [the phrase]." It'll request you to pronounce it properly and will register it for future use.

Make Use of the Camera's Depth of Field

Based on the ongoing rumors, iPhone 13 should feature a new and advanced 16 MP camera. It'll let you click exceptional pictures. With it, you can even catch the complete depth of the scene. To accomplish this, initiate the Portrait setting inside your camera and also have an up-close of the scene susceptible to catch the depth of field.

Established Music on the Timer

While training or taking a nap, many individuals play music in the background. However, this iPhone 13 novel function lets you play music on the timer as well. To accomplish this, go to the Clock>

Timer option. From here, beneath the "when the timer ends" characteristic, activate the burglar alarm for the decision of "End using." Whenever the timer strikes zero, it'll automatically turn off your music.

Make Quick Videos

Do you want to save a quick video for Instagram or share it with your friends? Instead of digging into the camera app to try and switch to video mode, just tap and hold the shutter icon to start recording a video with a quick shot on your 13 or 13 pro devices. Swipe right if you want to switch to video recording completely.

Photo in Apple ProRAW

Do you want to get the most out of your 13 pro device's camera? After that, you can shoot in ProRAW format.

This is Apple's approach to raw/dng, and it will provide you with additional options for post-production editing.

Get the MagSafe Portfolio Case With Find My Support

If you tend to lose your iPhone frequently, buy Apple's new MagSafe wallet case. Along with the iPhone 13, Apple has released an updated MagSafe wallet case with a built-in Find My support. This means you can track the case using the Find My app on your iPhone and other Apple devices.

The case can be useful if you can't track your iPhone directly. Instead, you can try to locate your wallet box.

Voice Web Search

Click on the tab bar at the lower part of the display screen and you'll see a receiver symbol that will show up at the most distant right of the text bar. Tap the microphone and you can dictate your search term for Siri. Once you're done talking, it will automatically search, so you don't have to press or type anything else. It is very useful.

Identify Animals, Articles, and Plants in the Photos

Your iPhone 13 and iPhone 13 pro would now be able to distinguish and give more data about a creature, milestone, plant, or item, just like a book. An icon is available above the photos in your gallery and with a simple tap, you can identify the breed of a pet dog and show more information, for example. Or you might name a flower with a background on the plant. The functionality is similar to that available on android phones called google lenses.

Use New Clothing Options for Memoji

If you love Memoji, you'll love the forty new outfits available for Memoji. In addition to new clothes, iOS 15 also features three different clothes colors, two different eye colors for the right and left eyes, new glasses, new stickers, and multicolored hats. Each one of the fresh qualities is accessible in the Memoji editor.

Tip on How to Make Use of Your Camera to Scan Texts

Have you at any point needed to face your device's camera on a map or piece of paper and have it naturally distinguish and duplicate the message to an email or archive?

Here is the place where live text sets in, and this new tip for the 13 and 13 pro models permits you to sweep and duplicate messages from iPhone photographs and cameras, regardless of whether it's manually written. And after extracting the text, you can paste it into any text field. It's incredible for rapidly sharing locations, numbers, and whatever else you would prefer not to type in with your fingers.

To use the new text scanning feature for iPhone 13 and iPhone 13 pro, press and hold in a text field as if you were going to use the copy and paste prompt. At this point, you will encounter a scan text console. You can also find a button that simply uses the scan icon, which looks like a piece of paper surrounded by brackets.

Tap the button that will replace the keyboard with the iPhone's camera viewfinder. Face your camera at the thing you'd like or need to check and adhere to the on-screen guidelines.

At the point when you appropriately adjust the camera and message, you will see a live highlight of the message distinguished by your iPhone and fit to be put in your archive. Click on the insert button when wrapped up.

Watch Videos in Picture-in-Picture Mode

Watch videos in picture-in-picture mode on the large screen of your iPhone 13 pro max. When you swipe up while watching a video in full-screen mode, the video should appear in a floating pip panel. Apps like Apple TV, Hulu, YouTube, and Netflix support the feature.

Change the Default Browser

You, at this point, don't have to possess Safari as the default program on your device or that of the pro model. All things being equal, you can set or place some other upheld outsider browsing programs like Chrome or Firefox, as the default program on your iPhone device.

To do this, go to the settings app on your iPhone 13 or iPhone 13 pro and select the app you want to set as the default. Then tap the default browser app and specify the default app.

Conclusion

You now have in your possession all the information you require to get the most out of your new iPhone 13. Try out each of these ideas to discover how effective they are for you. The iPhone has been a huge hit for Apple since its launch, thanks to its vast range of functions and great build quality.

The rear camera also features a significantly larger aperture of f/1.8, which is a significant upgrade over the iPhone 11's f/1.6 aperture. The rear cameras on the iPhone 11 and the Pixel 3 share the same f/1.8 aperture, but the iPhone 11 has a smaller sensor. As a result, it has more light, although it is less evenly distributed than the iPhone 13 camera.

Although the smartphone has a high price tag, it features a better display, a better camera, and a longer battery life.

Apple's new ProMotion technology is also included in the iPhone 13. A 12 MP pixel sensor replaces the earlier 16 MP pixel sensor in the iPhone 13 camera. So it's the same sensor as before, just with a different style of display. This signifies that the sensor's pixel size is the same as the front camera's pixel size. It also has a pixel size of 1.4m, which is the same as the Google Pixel 3. This implies the iPhone 13 camera can capture photographs with a lot of information and high quality.

The design of the iPhone 12 Pro has been upgraded slightly, although there are few modifications. The borders are stainless steel with a matte finish on the back and Apple's Ceramic Shield glass on both sides. The protection, according to Apple, makes the iPhone 4 times less likely to be broken than an iPhone without it.

Even though the Apple iPhone 13 is designed to be intuitive, understanding how to use the functions properly might be tough for the typical user. As you can see, this manual was written with this in mind, as it covers all you also need to know to get started with the iPhone 13.

To flawlessly handle your iPhone 13, it's crucial to keep in mind that the iPhone's touch screen will get dusty, especially around the edges and corners. As a result, it's critical to clean your iPhone with a microfiber cloth regularly. If you want to go all out, acquire the Apple Cleaning Kit, which will take care of everything for you.

As you can see, there are various tips and methods to help you take full advantage of your iPhone 13. You'll be able to get more out of your new phone if you spend more time learning about it. So make use of the information in this manual to get the most out of your smartphone and enjoy the extra perks that come with owning a top-of-the-line device!

You will be able to fully benefit from your new iPhone 13 smartphone if you carefully follow the directions in this User Guide. Follow the numerous short tutorials and explanations in this guidebook to learn about the iPhone 13's many impressive capabilities. You will appreciate your smartphone even more as you become more familiar with the different features and functions accessible on it. Thank you for purchasing the book and dedicating the time required to read it!

Manufactured by Amazon.ca
Acheson, AB